JusXtice ™

JusXtice ™

A TRAGIC AUTOBIOGRAPHY OF
ABUSE AND CRUELTY BY THE D.O.J

...

Iam Clarize

© 2017 Iam Clarize

All rights reserved.

ISBN: 1975913647
ISBN 13: 9781975913649

**Trademark applied
07/2017**

Dedication

My sincerest gratitude I give to my wife of over 50 years, whom I love dearly and to her sister, my son, and my two brothers who stuck with me through thick and thin. My old roommate and fraternity brother was there for me all the way, and to my closest in-town friends who prayed for me. I now believe that all their prayers contributed to my survival. And to our Italian sister, who also prayed and she was always there.
I cannot give enough praise to my dear friends as they have shown me the power of prayer. Through them, I received the strength to endure the ordeal and to keep going today.
Now to share with you and others what has happened to me and hopefully some changes will be made for the good.
It is by the grace of God that I was able to complete this book. May God bless them all and also may God bless all who suffer unjustly and may He give them peace.

"Human law is only law in virtue of its accordance with right and reason and this is manifested that it flows from eternal law. And in so far as it deviated from right reason it is called unjust laws in which such cases it is not law at all, but rather a species of violence."
St. Thomas Aquinas

Table of Contents

Acknowledgments xi
Personal Background xiii
Achievements xxi
I Am No Author - Only The Facts xxiii

Introduction 1
I Believed I Was Framed? 4
Welcome to My Hell for the Rest of My Life 11
Sentencing Transcript Statement 14
The Indictment 15
My Tragic Story 19
Transcript of proceedings before the judge 22
Arrest Detail 23
The Federal Court and my Sentencing 27
FBI Division Arrest 35
The Day of my Sentence 36
My Sentence and Conditions 41
Scanned Documents of my Sentence 42
Federal Court Fraternity 50
Overzealous Prosecutor 55

Out of my Element · 57
What Happens in the Courts Today · 60
Mens Rae · 64
Discovery · 69
Stacking · 73
Intended and Unintended Consequences · · · · · · · · · · · · · · · · · 75
Attorney Says No Trial · 77
Interstate and Intrastate Commerce Informaton · · · · · · · · · · 81
The Big Lie Made Under Severe Duress · · · · · · · · · · · · · · · · · · 85
Legal Blackmail · 88
My Assessment · 90
My Health Situation · 93
My Health History · 96
Health Problems · 101
My Physical Illnesses · 103
In Harm's Way · 107
Surveillance and Wire Tapping · 111
Stealing Your Social Security · 113
Retaliation · 115
Home Burglarized · 117
Friends and Foes · 120
I Have Been Abused and Screwed by my Government · · · · · 125
Prejudicial Court · 128
Mind Control within The Court · 130
Recidivism · 132
Norway's New System for Releasing Inmates into Society · · · 136
My Discussion - Life After Release · 141
Cost of Incarceration · 146
Parole · 148
Three Felonies a Day · 151

Born a Free Man but now a Slave 153
Good Morning Slave 157
From a Freeman to a Slave 161
Slavery - I Want to Die a Freeman 165
Slave – Yes, but How to Succeed 170
Mind Control - Introduction 176
Mind Control II - What is it? 180
Inmates 183
Disgrace 188
We Live Our Lives In Real Fear 191
I Shall Never Bow to Tyranny Again 195
There is No Life after Prison – Only Dispair 201
My Prison without Bars 206
Federal Bureau of Investigation 210
United States Marshal 212
Many Agree with Me 214
The Naked Truth 215
Why Me? 218
Check Your Prescription Medication Anomalies ... 219

Conclusion – The Bombshell 221
Thank You to my Wonderful Readers 223
Educational Sources 227

Acknowledgments

• • •

My wife, my partner, my friend, my lover and now my caretaker is a woman that I cherish and I love being around her 24/7. She is a phenomenal woman who has given me the impetus to write and especially finish this book. She also edited it for me, as she is a great editor, researcher and bibliographer. Since my ordeal, everything has been very documented. Facts do not lie.

I must thank others as I cannot use their names which is unfortunate. It is for their own safety. My wife's sister has been and still is so supportive that I owe a debt of gratitude that I can never repay.

My roommate and fraternity brother wrote to me inspirational letters that I needed for my own psyche. There are several close friends and neighbors who have not forsaken me. There is also my son, who I'm sure had his difficulties with the situation, and all will be fine. There is a friend we have adopted into our family, but lives in Italy, a beautiful, intelligent, compassionate woman that both my wife and I love and treat as our sister.

I also want to acknowledge all those who are suffering a similar fate that I have experienced. This is the big reason why I wrote this book. I do not expect anything to gain personally, but I hope that others may see some changes, for the good. This archaic system has been deprecating over the last 40-50 years and requires a serious intervention. The Department of injustice needs to go to rehabilitation.

I had what I thought to be wonderful friends that have forsaken me and I say unto them you are users and the hell with you. I do not need you or desire your friendship any longer.

May God bless you all.

Personal Background

• • •

I GRADUATED IN 1967 FROM an accredited university with a major in finance and minors in chemistry, sociology, philosophy and psychology.

While still in college I married my current and only wife. We have been married for over 50 years. And we are still together and we love each other dearly.

After I graduated from the university, I was employed by United States Steel as a management trainee. They had a training program that lasted two years after which time you were inducted into management. At this facility, they had new innovations for the making of steel, one of which was the BOP (Basic Oxygen Process). During my tenure as a trainee I was assigned to be the melter on several occasions. The melter takes 100 tons of hot metal (iron) and 100 tons of scrap metal and puts them in this large vessel that rolls back and forth on its trunnions. Then I placed the vessel in a manner to accept the scrap and hot metal on one side and on the other side the tapped liquid steel into a ladle for processing. Inserted into the vessel was a lance which introduced pure oxygen under high pressure that made 200 tons of prime steel in 32 minutes. On the backside of this unit was a continuous caster where I was placed and granted management status. I was the youngest trainee to ever receive management status. My time as a trainee was six months which was unheard of. I still had to complete my training, which was an exceptional management training program. I learned how to manage not only people, but also processes and procedures.

I transferred down to Baytown, Texas to start up the casters there and one day I was approached by my supervisors for a task. They told me that closed-bottom submerged pouring is the future of steelmaking as it makes the finest steel that is in demand today. There were 17 tubes specifically made for closed bottoms submerged pouring and I was given the task to make this process work, which many within the industry stated was impossible. They had a research facility in Pittsburgh, Pennsylvania and they could not get the process to work and I was given the impossible task. I accepted the challenge. To make a long story short, I was very successful. This was a project that was perceived to be doomed, but it is in use today all over the world. The solution was simple, but very elusive. One must persist and never give up, because a solution can be so close. One must believe in themselves.

While in Texas, we had a son who died when he was 2 ½. This is probably the most tragic thing that has happened to me in my life, and also my wife's. You may call me crazy or whatever you want, but I still talk to my son, especially when I am depressed. He brings me solace, and still today I grieve. I miss my son and always will.

If I loved him so much, how can I possibly hurt another child. At this moment, as I am writing to you, tears of sadness are falling from my eyes and onto my face. After 40 years, the pain is still within my very soul. I apologize for my misdirection, but you must know how I feel, and what I am really like in character. I am a peaceful man and for me to hurt someone or even thinking of hurting someone is an abomination. Sorry, I need to continue.

Our second son is now middle-aged and in good health. My second son also required surgery within weeks after birth. During the day, I went to work and I did my job, but at night I relieved my wife and I stayed with him all night. I did not sleep. This went on for three days and nights.

One time he broke his arm and I was in the hospital room when they were going to set his arm and place it in a cast. I heard a crack when they set his arm and I passed out. I guess I was just not strong to handle that situation, but that was my son. I was there to protect him. I did the best that I could.

When my son was growing up, he wanted to play hockey. That was fine with us, even though it is a very expensive sport. There was a lack of coaches, so I coached the small children hockey for several years.

For about seven or eight years, I coached soccer. My teams were comprised of both boys and girls of all ages and we were divisional champions many years, almost every year.

I loved working with the kids and watching them progress; to me it was a joy and a labor of love.

A short story, one of my soccer players was rather clumsy when it came to kicking the ball and participating within the sport. So, one year, I put in that left-wing, which is the scoring position. On the right wing, I had this power player, who would swoop in on the right and almost every time he made this swing he would attempt to make a goal and was relatively successful in doing such. I took this clumsy young man and put him on left-wing with very strict instructions. As soon as the right wing charged on the goal, he was to follow up behind him, as he always did not make that goal but the ball was loose and the goalkeeper was out of position and it was his job to kick that loose ball into the goal, scoring a goal. He scored many goals that season and he was a very proud young man and his attitude changed from one of I cannot do to one of I can do.

One day his father came up to me with this angry look on his face and he looked me straight in my eyes and told me that I cost him a lot of money this soccer year. I was amazed and asked him why? He said that he told his son at the beginning of the season that for every goal he scored he would receive $5. I knew nothing about this until he told me and he said that it cost him more than $100 Dollars. I laughed and smiled and told him, I wish you would've made it $10 instead of $5 per goal. I told him if I knew this prior to the season, he would have scored a lot more goals. He then smiled at me and we shook hands and he said thanks, and he stated that this gave his son confidence that he never had. It's moments like these that make one's efforts very satisfying.

To coach these children, I had to be licensed and I did have an F license. I am very proud of this license. Today I would much rather watch soccer and hockey than baseball, basketball or football.

I went through this long discussion of my steelmaking innovation for a reason, as I've had many technical challenges in my life, resulting in many successes. For one of these challenges I was called in as the last resort by a military manufacturing company which manufactured landing gear and fuel controls for military aircraft.

This company developed a unique circuit board which was made up of copper plate on both sides of the sandwich with an invar core in the shape of an alternating current power wave. This was the foundation so that two circuit boards could be attached, but this assembly had the same coefficient of thermal expansion as that of the to-be-attached polyamide board. The populated polyamide board was to be attached to both sides and utilized in the fuel control system for an F16. This was designed for weight reduction and to meet spacing requirements. The company spent over a million dollars to have this project and could not get it to work and I was the last resort to make it work or else the project would cease to exist, and $1.5 million of R&D was wasted. I had four weeks to complete my task, which included successful testing. The test was that this board must be still firmly attached after 500 full thermal cycles. The thermal cycle testing was 30 minutes at 120°F and 30 minutes at -40°F with a five-minute ramp between the upper and lower temperature requirements. I completed this supposedly impossible task in 3 ½ weeks.

In 1982, I got my first computer and I wrote a program that ran an inventory and billing system for a person's business. It ran for many years until he sold the business. I was involved with computers for the rest of my life including specifying and assisting in implementation of an enterprise-wide computer system that ran everything within the corporation. I also worked as a turnaround specialist where I would go into a company that was failing and turned it around and made it profitable. The company enjoyed success and employees usually ended up making more money.

I also garnered a patent when I was in my late 30s, which was a very difficult thing to accomplish, as the odds of ever getting a patent are insurmountable, but if one is determined enough one can accomplish the nearly impossible.

I cannot leave out one major aspect of my life, and that is my family. During my son's growth years through middle school and high school, he became attached to playing hockey which is a very expensive sport with a very long season. I took him to most of his practices and always to his games that my wife and I did attend. Many times, we had to travel several hours to another city for special games. Many times, this required overnight stays. I was always there for my family. My business and my jobs required a lot of attention, but never, ever, at the expense of my family. I was always there as I thought it was so important to guide my son with the correct disciplines to succeed. And my dear wife had plenty to do and she needed assistance with the house and I tried to be there for her, but a few times, travel took me away.

In my mid-60s, I decided to start my own business and designed a website with over 5,000 furniture items, by myself. I also started two distributing companies which sold hardware of many different types and varieties to retail customers, manufacturers and distributors. I had no other employees or personnel to assist in my endeavors. I created, maintained and drove these businesses and was just starting to blossom to where I could hire some assistance as I was working 14 to 16 hours a day, seven days a week, and I was exhausted. Then the FBI came knocking at my door and destroyed my entire life. I lost my company, I lost a lot of money, I lost a lot of my friends, where I was shackled to spend a large amount of time, I lost my health and became ill, sick and handicapped, all by the graciousness of the Department of injustice.

I worked long and hard hours to build my business. I worked 12 to 14 hours, sometimes 16 hours a day, seven days a week and when do I have time to mess around with such frivolous frivolity?

Even when I am not working I carry a pad and paper with me to jot down notes. To accomplish my goals, I did not do drugs or alcohol. In fact, I gave up drinking when I was in my 30's. And at my bedside, at night, I kept paper and a pen to jot down notes and ideas, as I would wake up during the night with an idea. The point being to all this is that I did not have the time to even think about what they told me I was supposed to have done and I was forced into the position that they created through their hostility, over-aggressiveness and above all to maintain their precious 96.8% conviction rate. By God, they will convict, no matter the intended or unintended consequences. Be DAMNED to the person that enters their courtroom, as a pig to slaughter, so goes the next candidate into their deadly playpen.

I do know that in the court record, the judge stated that he would look into Mens Rae, or my past to see if I had any criminal actions, but there was nothing in my past. Maybe his judgment would be different if he really did look, but somehow, I don't think it would be, nor did he apparently bother to look as he said he would. Call me cynical, call me whatever you want, but it is what it is.

It is said that there are three difficult things to achieve in life, as some say impossible. The three are: a doctorate, PhD or MD achievement, a patent, and writing a book. In my lifetime, I have accomplished two of the three impossibilities tasks. No, I'm not going to go after a doctoral degree. I'm going to write a couple more books and suffer the living Hell I was so unjustly delegated for the rest of my natural life.

I've had many achievements in my life, and I provide these in the next chapter. I did this to show you the type of person I really am and not what they say I was. My rights have been grossly misrepresented.

I live by this phrase that I have created.

"You can always question yourself many times over, but never ever doubt yourself."
The author

Achievements

• • •

<u>Some of my achievements during my lifetime</u>

- Assisted in re-railing derailed engines & trains on tracks
- Closed bottoms submerged pouring
- Double-sided polyamide board for fuel control system on F16
- Worked on Hummer assembly line with robotics and maintenance of machinery
- Preventive maintenance program for Hummer
- Revised production line for Jeeps for sale to Postal Service
- Systems analyst for several companies
- Developed automatic end-of-day procedure for next day's sales information
- Wrote a computer program for running of the company's inventory
- Garnered a patent on fireproof insulation
- Specified and assisted in implementing an enterprise wide computer system for a large company
- Turnaround of several companies from unprofitability to profitability

- Set up laminating department for production. Very successful
- Redesigned extrusion equipment for laminating department with significant savings on equipment
- Purchased the first new equipment ever purchased by large corporation. (CNC router). Success of first machine initiated more purchases. They said it could not be done
- Off-production operation - was told would fail, but was highly successful
- Pioneered with major corporation a new plastic product with significant lower TCE's
- Developed the first plastic trailer in the market
- Design award with the ASID (American Society of Interior Designers)
- Designed new furniture – especially tables.
- Started working when I was 11 years old
- Took apart and rebuilt lawnmower engine when I was 12
- Wrote a book and published
- Many times I was told of failure, but succeeded.
- Created, wrote, directed and filmed business videos. Training, orientation and sales promotion videos. I did this by myself
- Designed and built radical and revolutionary camping vehicle.

"You can always question yourself, but NEVER EVER DOUBT yourself"
Iam Clarize

I Am No Author - Only The Facts

• • •

I AM NOT AN AUTHOR or journalist, but I have written a few articles just for my own pleasure. Nor am I an attorney and I had no one to speak with regarding the legality regarding this book. I have taken it upon myself to explain the horrors that have fallen unto me and was shocked and still am in shock as to what happened, how and why it all happened, but more so what I have found out in my research, some things that will boggle your mind. What I am talking about here, me, is small in regards to what has happened and what will happen in the future. This unfairness within the justice system has been going on for over 45 years plus. You will have answers scattered throughout this book.

I am not going to sugarcoat anything, but to tell it from my perspective which is only the truth. Often, I will say, it has been very well documented as we kept meticulous records on a day-to-day basis as to what transpired.

At one time The United States had one of the finest legal systems in the entire world, which was based upon the British legal system. The British legal system today has not changed much over the years, but in United States it has changed drastically; it is rated in the world currently as one of the worst legal systems in the world.

The standard in the past was "you are innocent until you are proven guilty". Today that standard has changed to; "you are guilty and must defend yourself and prove your innocence". Plus, the caveat is, if you lose, the sentence is usually doubled.

Within the federal system, the court wins over 98% of its cases through plea bargains and duress. There are very few cases that go to court in which the defendant is set free. Plea bargains are the substance of the current judicial system and with very aggressive prosecutors and sordid evidence, these are easily obtained, which saves the court a lot of time so that they can prosecute more individuals to give to the loving care of the BOP. (*) The federal courts are known for their overzealous prosecutors.

I am writing this book knowingly that I might bear some consequences of retaliation. In other words, I could pay a heavy price for writing this book, and letting the truth be known.

Knowing this, I did not want to give up my name, but writing under a pen name I will be able to maintain some secrecy. I'm sure that anyone who really wanted to find me could find me. But then again, all I speak of is the truth. I do not slander or become libelous, just tell what happened as it happened.

For those that are in trials right now, or getting ready to go to this awful place called prison, maybe some things in this book will help. There are going to be several books of which book one is dedicated just to the judicial system and the second book will be dedicated to the BOP which has its own situations. The BOP is a very dangerous place, and for one who is older and has medical problems it is even more tenuous. I survived. I will tell you how

I survived in book 2 and I think you'll find it very interesting and unique. There are some good people within the institutions even though they have committed some heinous crimes. But the majority are not good people, and if you don't understand what you are doing, the consequences can be fatal.

In talking with psychologists and sociologists, they tell me that a geriatric male will more likely suffer from PTSD upon release, and in almost all cases, 100% of this population will suffer from this condition if innocent. Unfortunately, I do have PTSD and I am trying to get help.

So really learn, and I will be talking in the vernacular of those who speak such language. So, if your ears burn, put an ice pack on them, or give the book to somebody else.

It is what it is

Introduction

• • •

DURING MY LIFE, I HAD many challenges by the people that I worked for, people I worked with, and the hardest of all was creating things myself.

I never stopped working. Day or night, I'm either physically working, or mentally working. Wherever I go, I have a pad and pen with me for ideas and notes.

The pad and pen is my brain. It is my memory, my reminder and director.

THINKING OUTSIDE OF THE BOX

Many have heard this term over and over again, but I really do not think many of you understand the significance and how it really works.

Please let me try to explain how I look at this phenomenon. This is not an inborn trait, but rather a learned attribute, so each and every one of you can create.

Think of a football game at a large stadium.

You're on the playing field and are in the thick of the action, but the action you see is very little. You cannot see on the other side of the field, but only what is in your immediate area.

But let's go to the bottom seats of the stadium. Now you can see more and maybe you might even see down at one end of the field and see some scoring. But then again, you're limited, so let's go up to the nosebleed section and from here you get a view of everything that surrounds you as to what is transpiring on the field. Your vision is not limited but has expanded.

Oh, we are not done yet. We are going up in a blimp and now you can see everything that goes on around the stadium inside and out. Your view is expanded. To think outside of the box, you need to expanded your mind. Because you are not focused on one small area, but on a large area where you can gather information, ponder it, think about it and maybe something might strike you as an idea. You have to train your mind to broaden out.

The idea of this exercise is to not let your mind be focused on one small area. Rest assured you will not accomplish anything the first time, the second time, or even the 10th time, but there will be a time when suddenly it will happen. I guarantee it.

I was working at a company. I knew this gentleman there who wanted to learn how to think, as he was enthralled on how I got my ideas and solutions so quickly. I'm not anything special, I just train my mind to be special, that is all. And I digress… He kept coming at me with ideas, and I had to tell him no politely, that that would not work, but keep trying. When he came to me and said he had an idea, I always listened to him. He explained his idea and I stared at him for at least two minutes and he told me that was probably another dumb idea. I looked him straight in the eye and I said, "You finally did it. It's a great idea, and we're going to implement your idea immediately," and we did. He was proud of himself, but I was prouder of him for being persistent. After that period of time, he had more great ideas. Why? He expanded his mind. You too can expand your mind and don't stop trying.

What is the point of this discussion? Partially to tell you about myself. I have achieved many great things in my life and many were said to be impossible, but I succeeded.

It is not to brag, because it is just fact. I do not have the time, inclination, nor the intelligence to do what they say that I have done. I write this book, not for me, but for all the others who have been mistreated, abused, lied to and especially forced to take a plea bargain and as was said by the judge to forgo the expense of a trial. You will hear this term many times, it's all about the MONEY.

I Believed I Was Framed?

• • •

I WORKED HARD ALL MY life and the only times that I have done something wrong or against the law were confined to speeding and parking tickets, which were few. Never been to jail and always had the greatest respect for the law and I thought I was an upstanding law-abiding citizen, until this abomination happened.

I took my computers to be serviced by a company that manufactured and repaired computers, as my work was mostly done on the Internet, as one of my companies sold products on the Internet. I needed a company that would service my computers. This computer maintenance company installed, at their insistence, a system that backs up all my data in real time. So, if I lost a hard drive I was to simply swap drives, then the program would rebuild the data if lost by the failed hard drive failure. This process is called RAID. This way I would have peace of mind that all my data was intact in real time.

My company was starting to become successful. I sold furniture over the Internet, with high profit margins and high-quality goods. I did all the web work myself and got myself a high ranking within Google. If that's not enough I also had a distributorship selling knobs like kitchen knobs to the RV industry and another distributorship also selling goods to the RV industry. I also sold products retail but not on the Internet, but through other techniques.

I was in my late 60s at the time with several health issues which caused me a lot of problems, but yet I worked anywhere from 10 to 14 hours a day, seven days a week. I did all the sales, marketing, pricing, ordering; anything that needed to be done, I did. After four years of continuous hard work and expenditures of quite a bit of money, my company was finally giving me a return on my investment. And once it was set up, it would be very easy to run.

This is where the trouble started.

I hired the wife of my accountant, a CPA. I have known them for years and he took care of my personal and business taxes. But he had nothing to do with my businesses or previous businesses I owned. I consulted with businesses owners, and I became a turn-around specialist by which I would, through a series of different methodologies, make the business profitable. Some people might have some technical skills, such as accounting, but cannot grasp the whole picture behind running a business, since numbers are a big factor pertaining to the business, but that's only about 15% to 20% of what is required in a knowledge base to run a successful business.

My accountant had tried his hand at business and had a franchise selling a certain type of baked goods in a mall setting. The product was delicious. Something happened, and the business was no longer there. He would not tell me why the business closed, but I can guess. He was good at keeping books, and pushing numbers around, but I feel he must not have had the slightest idea how to run a business, with all its nuances, problems and interactions.

Also, tragedy fell upon the family in that one of his son's daughter was born prematurely. At his insistence, and not the family's, they tried to save the child's life and by some miracle the child survived, but not because of him; she thought he was the savior.

We lost a son when he was 2 ½ and he knew about this and of course I had a lot of empathy for him and tried to help him in all the ways that I could, but he was of his own mindset and he would not listen. This was a difficult time for me, as memories of my son bring forth memories and still today I seriously grieve his loss. Losing a young child of your own to me has been devastating. I have a special fondness for children. That's why this crime was over creatures that had been condemned on me. Forgive me, but this was a very hard thing to write about.

My accountant used to call me for my counsel, and I found out that he's quite the basket case in more ways than one. I did tell him several times to keep his nose in his own business, as everyone was against what he was wanting to do, and he was very disappointed in my reactions. He could not handle the truth.

During his time of mourning, he used to talk to my wife. He would tell my life, and later me, that he was a member of the United States Special covert Ops and that he traveled the world on United States government business and bragging about playing soccer with the Pope. He was apparently not deep ops, but still in the secret part of the government. He stated that he has earned 16 Medals of Honor for his service. My wife told me of his past, and I was quite skeptical. In times of grief people can make up stories. But he was also a researcher probing into the death of John Kennedy. And he had a lot of Kennedy memorabilia around his house. He later told me that he was involved with special government operations.

His wife's father passed away, and we went to the funeral and also visitation at the funeral home. In looking at the flowers, there was a bouquet from each of the living Presidents of the United States, including Ronald and Nancy Regan, and one bouquet from us. He told us there would be no speaking at the service, but he got up in front of everybody and babbled for over 20 minutes and prior to his eulogy, he placed on his father-in-law's casket something that may have been or looked like a Medal of Honor, as he told it was a real Medal of Honor.

Then one evening, I received a phone call from him, asking me for $37,500, and that he needed the money quickly to pay off a debt regarding his grandchild, or put a bit in his business. He said that he would do my taxes for the rest of my life. He said if I said no, there would be no hard feelings, and I said no. Maybe, I was naïve.

I had my accountant's wife do my business books and pay my bills, because I just did not have time. I needed help. She was to be the only one involved in this business, but I believe my accountant had his eyes on a bigger prize, my business.

I cannot prove that he was after my business, but after I was incarcerated my wife did prove that he was embezzling funds from my company, and doing things with the company's money that he was not authorized to do. We had a professor of finance go through my entire books and proved that he was embezzling funds from my company. My wife took this information to the police, and they did nothing. She took it to the Northern Indiana Attorney General, and he did nothing. This guy must have some pull someplace to get away with this. Things like this are going around a lot, people getting away with things and they are federal offenses, while others go to jail for hardly any reason at all.

Was he part of the ruination of my life? I have not been able to prove the fact that he set me up? I have been trying to find out if there is a relationship between him and the owner of the computer service company. Also, he's had some discussions with the judge, and I do not know what the discussions were about and if I knew, I do not think I would like the answer, because he is high on my list of someone who might want to put me in jail for many reasons. A son of my former accountant is a prominent attorney on the West Coast.

While incarcerated, my wife came down to visit with me one weekend, and our house was broken into and a lot of jewelry and money was stolen. (*) I believe that this was a professional hit, and some things about the act are suspicious, such as in my desk drawer were two packages of Fentanyl I use for my pain. These were not taken. But, there was an incident in which there was a call on my wife's cell phone originating from the Regional Medical Administrator's office of the federal facility in which I was housed, and the phone number and this man's name were on the sim card. We feel they were looking for this card. Research has shown us that the prefix of the telephone number, as well as the phone number, is a government number. We feel that this was a professional hit, maybe somebody local, or more likely the BOP, who was harassing me and this is their form of retaliation. There are more details on this subject in another chapter.

My accountant wrote my wife a letter, stating that he had pancreatic cancer and that it was historically 98% fatal. So, to lessen part of his practice he advised us, and we were one of the first to go, to contact one of his buddies. His buddy was no better than he was, but that's another story. Suddenly, out of the dark and misty night, he was cured, not in remission, but cured. Is this a miracle? Or was it a blatant lie? (*)

He must've really hated me, because he called my son, and tells him to watch over his back, because the same thing could happen to him. What a cruel heartless thing to do to someone. This just goes to show what type of person he really is. (*)

Some outside hands had to be involved in this caper, because the numbers really are quite small, and where they found it was in the bowels of the computer where the actual programs reside. I have worked with computers since 1982, and feel anyone who stores information or other material within the bowels and programs of the computer is a complete idiot and for a service company to do this, there must have been a lot of hatred involved or stupidity or my guess is and always will be a set-up.

I have heard from others that my former CPA is still working as an accountant. As far as what I think about his involvement? You know the answer and I do not have to tell you what I feel, but the proof is there. I spent three years in a federal prison, where the medical department did not treat me properly, but, harassed me, used retaliation and invoked cruel and unusual punishment, possibly made possible by my accountant.

What might I do about him? I will let God take care of this miserable, wretched, despondent poor excuse for a human being.

It is time to go forward.

It is not until this past year that I was aware of all the issues involved with my old accountant and his various goings-on while I was incarcerated. He had been using my company to pay his telephone bills for over three years, including calls overseas, on subject matter of which I was totally ignorant, and I would not condone such contact with some of the people he called. My wife noticed this activity after I told her to get the company records after I was incarcerated. Monies were taken out of the company for their personal gain. This was reported to the county and governmental people without any action taken whatsoever.

Something is wrong. He was using my company, without my permission, for activities of which I was unaware. Perhaps these activities could be illegal; I sincerely believe he set me up in the first place, to use my company without permission. (*)

Then I get the highest possible sentence available without just cause. Something is very wrong here.

Meticulous records have been kept, and will be distributed to other parties who may take action into what seems to be an illegal operation. And I was the dupe, who now has a record, a slave to the government, and worst of all, innocent of all charges and fully believing that I was set up for the fall if anything went wrong.

We are now again expecting retaliation, unless we get protection, which I doubt and I cannot have a gun to protect myself and my wife, and there have been some incidences of some crazies throwing rocks at my house and this disturbs me deeply. Why must an innocent man suffer such as I, for the rest of my life?

I CANNOT DEFEND MY FAMILY BECAUSE OF THE RIDICULOUS ASININE REQUIREMENTS DEMANDED OF ME.

HOW WOULD YOU FEEL IF YOU WERE IN THIS ENVIRONMENT?

As I am finishing up this book, a very strange thought comes into my mind as now I begin to wonder if this culprit that I do believe has set me up belongs to such groups as the Club of Rome, or other nefarious deeply secret organizations. Something smells, and it is not roses.

It is what it is

Welcome to My Hell for the Rest of My Life

• • •

"No longer is it, one is innocent until proven guilty, but now you are guilty and must prove your innocence." (*)

THE AUTHOR

AN OFFICIAL WITHIN THE JUSTICE Department said to me that I was charged, sentenced, and convicted for a crime of what I MIGHT do. One must commit a crime and be proven with facts for it to be valid, and my crime was not proven or factually shown that I committed one.

I was charged and convicted of a heinous federal crime that I did not commit. The justice system uses its power, might and overwhelming superiority to convict anyone that crosses their threshold. If you are within their grasp, your only resort is to plead out. Trying to prove your innocence is not only very expensive but futile. You will lose and pay a price for trying. (*)

Today I am a 73-year-old man, very sick, and with cancer and many other illnesses and a lot of my current conditions are the direct result of being incarcerated and not having proper medical attention. Today I suffer with illnesses and am always in pain, lots of pain. A listing of my illnesses will be supplied later in this book.

The only crimes that I committed in the past were for a few speeding and parking tickets. I always followed the law as best I could, as best as anyone can, but you will see in this book, you are a loser. Yes, you will be a loser.

When I served out my time, I was a broken man. They did little to help my illnesses while I was incarcerated, even though I was in a medical facility. This medical facility is touted as being one of the finest in the country, but they practice minimalistic medicine, which is only to provide the medications and other necessary items just to keep you alive so they can collect their MONIES.

While incarcerated, I was chastised, rebuked and punished for things I did not do. I was retaliated against and our home was robbed while my wife was visiting me. (*) I sincerely believe that this action was carried out by government people as I feel they were looking for something that could embarrass them. There is no use to sue them, as they own the courts. We have tried to get action on a crime committed against us, with documentation, and were turned away. That is another reason why I am writing this book, because there is no justice, just injustice.

Do I fear for my life? The answer is yes, I do! (*) They can even do worse things to me, but now that the book is written they can do what they want, as my telling you the truth will set me free. And freedom is such a precious gift and if that was taken away from you, you would understand what freedom really means.

All of my former friends except for a very few close friends have left me. I have one brother who will not talk to me, so I say unto him, bro, go fuck yourself, but on the other hand my other two brothers have been marvelous and as for my friends in the states and overseas, I cannot thank them enough for their support, their love and their prayers. I strongly believe that their prayers sustained me through my torturous ordeal. There are also my neighbors who are all very kind unto me and I sincerely thank them.

You may not agree with everything I say, but that's your problem. There's a saying in prison, "it is what it is" and share my trials and tribulations.

It is what it is

(*) This is a symbol which the author uses to show he believes this to have some significance

Sentencing Transcript Statement

• • •

TRANSCRIPT OF PROCEEDINGS BEFORE THE judge (name not to be mentioned)
April 19 2012
Pages 47 – 48

THE COURT (judges speaking name not to be mentioned)

> "the statute that you violated allows a sentence of anything from zero to 10 years. Those are the possible sentences I can impose, anything in that range."

The Indictment

• • •

I was brought in front of the judge to give my plea of not guilty to the court. The indictment of which I was accused was for the intent to view child pornography. The bond was set for $10,000, of which the court was going to pay, and I was set free.

I found out that the federal government contacted the state for participation within this trial, and they refused. (*) (*) I believe they saw no merit, but the feds probably had little to do and needed someone to be convicted of a crime (business must have been slow). They need to keep the pipeline filled so as they can collect the monies. As you will hear often enough, it is all about the MONEY.

I was called back into court and was promptly arrested, thrown into jail, stripped of all my clothes and sent into a cell naked with only two blankets. (*) The bed consisted of a steel slab with no mattress. I was in excruciating pain without my pain patch for back surgery in the past. I was rousted every three hours, and had to leave the cell naked and stand out in the hallway in front of all the other incarcerated individuals, while they went into the cell to make sure there was no contraband or anything that I could do myself harm because I was placed on suicide watch, which was totally ridiculous and absurd.

I cannot commit suicide because I had a small taste of it, as it was induced by a medication that I had taken in the past. My doctor said that I was suffering from depression many years in the past and told me that I needed to take these antidepressant medications. I rebelled, but forces were against me and so I took them. About four days after taking this medication, I told my wife to go and hide my guns from me, as I was having hallucinations of committing suicide. Believe me, it was a very enticing proposition, but then I realized, very bluntly, that if I did such, there is no way back and immediately destroyed that idea forever. I love my life and would not cause any harm. My doctor then tried again with another drug and the same thing happened. This was at a time when this adverse reaction to these medications was not known and I became an advocate to make this deleterious side effect known.

To be released from this servitude of a suicide watch, one must be released by a psychologist who visits the facility for just this reason and normally that's a period of three days. I was held there for seven days in this position and my wife pushed on to get me off of this suicide watch. She contacted another attorney who was able to gain my release from jail.

But I had just gotten the first taste of being in the HOLE or SHU (special housing unit), and for the rest of the time that I was incarcerated within the county jail (*) I was held in this horrible format. You are alone, and while I was under this suicide watch they would put a tray through the door, and I had to eat the food with my fingers and the food was awful.

This county jail that I was in was relatively new, but what an awful place in so many ways. Most of the guards appear to be masochistic, the food is a rendering of sub-garbage, not to be compared to the gourmet feast that one would get out of a dumpster. (*)

I digress....

This was my first taste of being incarcerated and getting the treatment that I did; I do not blame the officers, as they were doing as they were trained. Some are a little bit more aggressive than others, but it's all in management and I do blame them. There are a lot of bad people in the county jail and strong actions have to be taken to not only keep them from hurting themselves but also from hurting others. So, at times, force must be taken and I understand that, but my problem is mostly with the attitude of a few. Example: I was standing at the desk where you are interned. I put my hand on the desk. He told me to keep my hands off of HIS desk. I informed him that this was not his desk but that of the taxpayers, after which I received a serious barrage of angry words, and what he would do to me if I did not shut my pie hole. (*) I placated of course, but I will never forget the incident as I will see this attitude carried forth through the rest of my holiday as a guest of the Federal Injustice Department.

This was my first experience with any judicial system and it sucks, especially when you are innocent.

I was finally let out, and was supposed to have a meeting within a short period of time but that never happened. The rules started changing and the techniques started to be different, and I did not know one thing from another of what's to happen.

The sentencing will be made known in the next couple of chapters.

If you have never been arrested or put in this position before you cannot understand how difficult it is to even cope with what is going on, especially when there are several individuals of high rank there messing with you.

The courts were initially set up in an adversarial nature, where the defense attorney was your friend and ally. Of the three attorneys that I had, they were more attuned to the prosecution's side. More on this later as you will find it probably interesting.

It is what it is

My Tragic Story

• • •

AT THE WRITING OF THIS book I am 73 years old and in very poor health due to the lack of acknowledgment of basic medical treatment by the Department of Injustice {DOI}, which is comprised of several different entities: The Marshals, the FBI, the persecutor, the judges and the Bureau of Prisons or BOP.

I was quite ill when I discovered that I was a candidate for certain punishment for a crime for which I cry innocence to this day. Once you are targeted by the FBI, you will lose and eventually go to jail unless you are part of the political elite as you will see in the current news. The rest of us poor bastards suffer any consequences they wish to impose upon us.

Money, time and personnel are on their side. I was led to believe many years ago "you are innocent until proven guilty". But now the parameters have changed and now the policy is "prove your innocence", and if you lose the trial, your sentence will be doubled, and that is illegal as it is called stacking. That may have been changed now because they got caught not obeying the law and what was their punishment, nothing, nada and free as a bird. But for us, we become slaves of the United States government after we have served our term within the BOP as prescribed by the judge.

Okay I am not a journalist, writer, or author, but I must tell this story. This is the real life as it was and is today.

Nothing will be sugarcoated, and foul language might be used at times for emphasis, but that is real life. But I do have a major fear. The writings in this book are all factual and can be backed up as we have kept detailed notes and logs of everything that has transpired to me since the first eventful day. A lot of time and effort has gone into this blunder by the government, as it is a blunder. There are so many mistakes and errors that were committed, and I suffered severe consequences not only by jail time, but a severe downgrade of my health, as I suffer every day. Do they care, fuck no; maybe over their possible little parties at noon and having their scotches, while I was incarcerated, having rice for lunch. I hate rice now and I hate chicken as that is all we seemed to get while "relaxing at the resort."

I am suffering from PTSD and have been since before leaving prison. I have yet to get proper treatment for this condition and I'm still trying to get help. But I am reminded every day of the horrors of my past life and the huge disservice that this injustice did to me.

I believe the purpose of this is because of an action I took in having the persecutor and my attorney sign a document that I would not go to jail after meeting with the magistrate. And the magistrate was pissed. I know that the judge chastised both the persecutor and my attorney as I was supposed to go to jail. Then I believe the magistrate is chastised by the Court, therefore creating prejudice against me and did everything in their power to make me suffer. Just because of a little ass chewing they take out unconscionable punishment on a person. Shame on them. They certainly are not members of the human race, wonder what they are?

How does one individual compete against these forces? I have not the power to do anything, nor do I have the energy anymore to fight as I would have if I was healthy. I know I live in a very small world, with hardly any friends, but I have my charming and loving wife who stood by me for 50 years, and I just love being around her as she makes me forget the horrors and the persecution and the indignation and retaliation that I have received during this fateful and miserable time.

The purpose of this book is to educate others, as I am doomed to a life that I will live for the rest my life as was imposed by this vicious judge whom an attorney said, "He is not known for his compassion." I wonder what he will say when he reads this and I doubt if he will read this.

Transcript of proceedings before the judge

(name not to be mentioned)

• • •

April 19 2012
Pages 47 – 48

THE COURT (judge speaking name not to be mentioned)

"the statute that you violated allows a sentence of anything from zero to 10 years. Those are the possible sentences I can impose, anything in that range."

I GOT 4 YEARS. YOU DECIDE…
It should not be what it is

Arrest Detail

• • •

Appendix 1
XXXXXXXX—The United States Attorney's Office announced today that:

Pleas
XXXXXX, 68, of XXXXXX, pled guilty before Magistrate Judge XXXXXXXXX to the felony offense of intent to view child pornography.

The investigation began when XXXX took his computer into a local business for repair work. In the process of working on the computer, a juvenile employee of the business noticed what he believed to be pornographic images of girls who were underage. The employee further observed a large amount of data in various folders containing the same sort of material. Law enforcement was contacted and pursuant to a search warrant, a forensic search was conducted which allegedly uncovered approximately 576 images and 22 videos depicting child pornography.

Sentencing has been set for XXXXX

This document will be shown to you in its entirety as appendix 1 at the end of this book, so that you can see the actual numbers. I have blocked out the names to protect the guilty and the innocent.

It is important to note that there was no commitment of any kind that proved that I had viewed child pornography. It is only a complaint of intent that I might do so. This is the same thing as saying I am going to shoot somebody and given the time & place of this event. By law, I am not guilty of anything because I have not committed the crime. Now if I went to this place and actually did the deed that I said I was going to do, I am certainly guilty, but only then when the action has been completed can the occurrence be assessed. It is also my belief that I was extremely pressured to take a plea because they did not want to have the involvement of the service required within a possible trial. So, in order to facilitate my taking a plea, they upped the ante to force me and brought all the pressure they could bear to make it happen. Unfortunately, they were successful. Knowing what I do today, it would not happen. That is because I was ignorant, dumbfounded, bullied, harassed and coerced into taking a plea. This is why I am so upset, and many other people who are innocent of their crimes are and should be upset too.

I contend that the service company I took my computer to could have put these images on my computer and called the police. I have no way of proving this action, as I am sure if it was done, they would remain quiet. It is also interesting to me that the son of the former sheriff of our county just happened to be the manager of this computer firm. Also, the person who did the initial examination of my computer was a "juvenile" (in records) who later became a manager at this same firm.

Judging guidelines have been set up by a commission that has made sentencing guidelines for all judges to follow. The judge supposedly has final discretion over these guidelines.

Notice that the number of images and videos was noted, but at sentencing somehow the number was greatly increased. What is going on here? Within the sentencing guidelines the original number of images and videos has a very low sentence, or possibly even none. My research has shown that the number of images and videos is a really insignificant small amount to the large number of images that would be conducive to my severe punishment (*)

So, what has happened? I believe I have the answer. I might be wrong, but I think not. What has happened is the illegal precedent of stacking was invoked. The sentence was escalated higher than the original indictment. My sentence is egregious, as it does not follow the original indictment. There is not much I can do about this because, when you plead guilty, you do not have any legal rights for an appeal. **(I pled guilty under coercion because they said if I went to trial and did not win, my sentence would be doubled and as my attorney said he would not defend me, so I lose.)** One can hardly do anything while incarcerated and even having a great person like my wife trying to assist me, getting answers from the attorneys in our local area was next to impossible. We have the good old boys club within this judicial community and each member of this club is very careful about whose toes they might step on. Mistakes are covered over. But, I can do little, because I do not have access to any attorneys within this community **whom I trust**, so this is one of the reasons why I am writing this book, which is to show you my dear readers, that

25

you must be very careful if the eyes of the FBI ever fall upon you. Learn all you can to protect yourself and try to give yourself a few insights as to what really goes on.

There is a more definite answer for you as to why this happens and I will share that with you much later in this book, and I think you'll find it quite fascinating.

It is what it is

The Federal Court and my Sentencing

• • •

THE COURTROOM ITSELF IS SPECIALLY designed to give the impression of total control and to demonstrate their perceived unlimited power over life and death to those charged with a crime. These are the guardians of our legal system whose decisions affect millions of people. The judges have no accountability. They answer to no one. They are not even elected. They are politically appointed by those who are in power at that time. They usually come from generations of families of attorneys. In my mind's eye, they have a very limited scope of the real world. They really do not know, on a personal basis, how you and I live, struggle and to make do with the best that we can. This is not to pick on them, but it's only to state a fact of the real world.

Millions of peoples' lives are at stake with the decisions made up by a small amount of people. Yes, you heard me correctly, millions of people, as their decisions not only affect that one person being incarcerated, but his family and those that depend upon him for guidance, security, money and especially for the nurturing of the children, which everyone seems to forget about. Let us not forget that the male part of the family is traditionally the disciplinarian and as he goes, children go. The old adage "like father, like son" was so prevalent, and we forget this basic fact, which in turn causes many more problems.

The children no longer have a father figure as he was also taken away with other government projects for the purported betterment of society, but the unintended consequences were overlooked which ended up destroying the families, the basis of our society. I could go on and on and on about the injustices, but rest assured I will discuss this in more detail later.

I was condemned as a criminal and was getting ready to go to trial but had to give a guilty plea under extreme duress. That is my story and I'm sticking to it. Four individuals controlled my destiny for the rest of my life. They are the magistrate, the judge, the persecutor and of course, my worthless attorney. It is off to the kangaroo court for their dispersal of punishment for a crime I did not commit, and if you understand this law, it makes absolutely no sense.

In all my 73 years, I always observed people, as they tell me a lot about their personalities. In this case, I just want to share some of my thoughts with you. Obviously, they're all factual and possibly anecdotal.

I do not really know what the magistrate does, but to sit on his high dais of highly polished wood, playing his role of man God, dispensing something, as it certainly is not justice.

The Judge:
The judge is supposedly the leader of the court however he is heavily influenced by the overzealous prosecutors. His main function is just to keep some semblance of order within the courtroom and

to maintain a calendar. He also was supposed to take in all the facts: such as recommendations by the parole office, and the recommendations received from the accused's families and friends, and the most important thing of all is to conform to the laws dictated by the Congress of The United States. The judge is not to change, bend, or amend and is to follow the normal course of a trial such as giving to the defendant all the benefits of the doubt. The judge is responsible for looking into Men's Rae and finding any possible criminal activities within the accused's past life, to look into his age and status of health. The judge flunked in this area, big time.

The judge is also to make sure that the defendant has participated in discovery. This is the key element in facts leading to his potential sentence, if he is guilty. Again, the judge flunked. We have proof that no discovery was given to me for evaluation.

Congress has passed a law that stacking is illegal and no sentence shall be stacked. What does this mean? Stacking is the adding of additional time to the initial sentence for other crimes that may have been committed, but not necessarily have been taken to trial. Stacking in my case was the creation of many images from the few they found. An image can only be used one time and if that image is on several different drives, still, this is only one image. So, the images that I was initially charged with somehow escalated to a phenomenal amount. This is a very strong hypothesis from what I know of the statute regarding sentencing guidelines. My interpretation of the sentencing guidelines based upon the number of images that I initially know about, that's all I know about could in fact, be thrown out of court. The judge flunked again.

There is more, that's enough you get the point that this judge was not a benevolent judge, but actually was the voice box of the persecutor.

Magistrate:

I used to work out in a rather exclusive gym. Anyone can join, one just needed money and much more than the other gyms requested. Most of these gym members were attorneys, politicians, doctors, businessmen and others of the community. It is a nice informal gym where everyone called each other by their first name, and conversations were very sociable.

I did know of him at this time, but the magistrate joined the club and I just cautiously observed him, but never spoke to him as I did not know he was the magistrate, but only from some court system. After some rather short period of time members were calling him by his first name. He would immediately chastise them and tell them that he was a judge and he was to be called, "His Honor" or "Your Honor". Actually, hearing this for myself, I knew that I would never have any contact with this individual, as well as did the other members. Those that used to change clothes near him went to the other side of the locker room.

Persecutor:

You have heard stories of aggressive prosecutors. Well mine was one on an overdose of steroids. He was a combination of an angry pit bull, a crazy mastiff and a frenzied ape. He will do anything to see that those before him go to prison, but just not me, everyone he is charged to prosecute, he will send them to prison.

This court as I am told by FBI and the Marshals, has a winning ratio of 98.6%. They lose very few cases. And as I was told by my attorney they will use every dirty trick in the book to assure them of the win, and make up some of their own. (*)

My research has shown that usually the prosecutor in the system makes more money than the judge. They are graded on their aggressiveness and of course their win ratios. The state however usually only has about a 50% to 60%-win ratio. At least one stands a chance in the state court, while in the federal court, just kiss your ass goodbye.

Attorney:

A message was delivered to me by my attorney telling me of this success ratio and the lengths that the prosecutor will go through to obtain the conviction, so it's best that I take a plea no matter what it might be. But the next words out of his mouth were that he will not defend me in court as he stated he cannot beat this man in court because he is more powerful than he. (*) Yes, my attorney said this; at that moment I knew I was screwed. My attorney also stated that if I did go to court and lose, my sentence would be doubled. This procedure is called stacking and has been in use in the judicial system for many years and from what I hear it is illegal. And I have known many inmates who are incarcerated for long lengths of time due to stacking of their sentence. Supposedly this is now illegal once again, but it was illegal before, until Congress caught up with them.

When I talked to my third and court-appointed attorney that I had who was on the Criminal Justice Panel, he talked about how expensive it is to send his kids to a Catholic grade school, how long he has to wait to get his check for his services, but nothing to defend me. It was always about him. He did tell me that he would work a special deal out with the prosecutor and has been very successful with this in the past and keeps reminding me of this one drug dealer in Chicago that he got off with a very minimal sentence as his only claim to fame.

One would think of a person of reasonable intelligence would fire him. I would have but I had acquired two other attorneys previously, and the judge appointed this attorney to me and told me that I better work with this attorney because otherwise there would be instant sentencing. This is what they do. They demonize you, and if I knew better, as I do today, I would have told him I wanted to go pro se, and he would have to honor that commitment. Then at this time I believe that I would have been spared because of the circumstantial evidence against me. That is the basis of the entire suit against me: a hypothetical that I might, just MIGHT commit the crime. (*) (*) They use a rope a dope, and I was a dope, and I fell for it every bit. But this is their mantra, submit you to so much stress that you cannot clearly think rationally and forever suffer the consequences, as I am doing. I digress. I will talk about this a bit later.

Sentencing

Research has shown that my judge graduated from law school, got his degree and worked in the private sector for a very short period of time, as his family was connected within this judicial fraternity. He was made a judge very early on after his schooling, and allegedly learned the easy life of a judge and committed himself to taking advantage. I was positioned.

At my sentencing, he was 45 minutes late. He came in the courtroom happy as a lark telling us of the wonderful time he had accepting some kind of honor for doing something. The amazing thing was that he was not one bit ashamed of his tardiness, but rather he appeared to be bragging. (*)

He allowed a friend of mine to speak on my behalf, only was rather short with him. My attorney was to give closing remarks and as he told me the day before, he had not even started his closing, and I had to literally write it for him at that time.

When the judge was asked if he read the letters of recommendation for me, he scurried around his desk and he could not find them and stated that he did not read them because he did not have them. The parole officer stated that they were sent to him for his review. When asked if he read the probation recommendations, he said he glanced at them. The recommendation of the parole office was for three years' home confinement, because of my illnesses. (*)

I was given the opportunity to talk and was interrupted by a bombastic prosecutor several times during my dissertation, and the judge even had to tell him to back off and let me speak. I spoke of my illnesses, in particular of my multiple myeloma cancer, which is a disease of the immune system. Multiple myeloma is a rare, very painful and deadly cancer. At that time, there was no conclusive method of remission. Regarding my cancer, I went to the Indiana University Hospital in Indianapolis for a second opinion regarding the progression of my multiple myeloma. After some testing, it was confirmed that I did have smoldering multiple myeloma. I then offered myself to participate in a clinical study, but was told at that time there were no studies being conducted.

The judge seemed quite happy to pronounce my sentence. He sentenced me to 48 months, lifetime supervised probation and five years of special counseling, with two days per week of individual sessions and one session per week of group therapy. (*) This, according to others, was an egregious sentence, and I will explain to you all the nuances and legal abuse that I found out about after my release. I will share this information with you in several chapters.

It bothers me even today that the judge did not read the letters of recommendation or give any credence to the recommendation of the parole office, as they did a lot of work on my case. He did no work on my case as he said that he would do. It is still my contention that he could send his secretary to give the verdict, and he could sit back in his office remonstrating his recent moment of glory at the elongated luncheon. You will understand my bitterness, as this was no legal trial by any means, but one of a kangaroo court. (*)

I probably will get repercussions of my last comments, but as I stated before, facts are facts, and that is how this transpired, especially when I still claim my innocence today. If something should happen to me, the facts, still remain the facts and there is no way around that, except for lies.

It is what it is

FBI Division Arrest

• • •

Attorney's Office
The United States Attorney's Office announced today that:

Pleas
pled guilty before Magistrate Judge to the felony offense of possession of child pornography. The investigation began when he took his computer into a local business for repair work. I n the process of working on the computer, an employee of the business noticed what he believed to be pornographic images of girls who were underage. The employee further observed a large amount of data in various folders containing the same sort of material. Law enforcement was contacted and pursuant to a search warrant, a forensic search was conducted which uncovered approximately 576 images and 22 videos depicting child pornography.

The Day of my Sentence

• • •

Transcript of proceedings before the judge

THE COURT (judge's speaking name not to be mentioned)

> "the statute that you violated allows a sentence of anything from **ZERO** to 10 years. Those are the possible sentences I can impose, anything in that range."

AT MY SENTENCING, THE JUDGE was 45 minutes late. The judge came into the courtroom dressed in his freshly pressed black robe, happy as a peacock and he was telling us of the wonderful time he had at a very long lunch getting some kind of honor for doing what or whatever, I do not know. The amazing thing was, that he was not one bit ashamed of his tardiness, but rather he was a braggadocio as the court had to wait for him. What would happen if I was late? I find his actions disgusting, reprehensible, and basically uncouth. (*) I wonder if he had been drinking? If this was the case, he should have made another court date.

A friend of mine travelled from Chicago, Illinois to speak on my behalf, but I feel the judge belittled him and treated him with disdain. I could tell from his antics this was off to a lousy start. If I were a judge, I would have held him in contempt in my court and thrown his ass in jail to cool down. This was getting out of hand. This is the way I was feeling about my perilous situation, and I was in peril.

My attorney gave the worst closing remarks I have ever heard. He was not prepared, as I had to write it for him the previous evening. He was digging my grave. Instead, I should have not assisted him and made him look like an ass. Even with my assistance, he could not remember half the things that I told him to bring up. It was dry and without merit and when I heard his comments I just stuck my head between my legs and kissed my ass goodbye. (*)

When the judge was asked if he read the letters of recommendation for me, he scurried around his desk and he could not find them and stated that he did not read any of them because he did not have them. The parole office stated that they were sent to him for his review a week prior. When asked if he read the probation recommendations, he said he glanced at it. The recommendation of the parole office was for three years' home confinement because of my illnesses. (*) Now here's my life on the line and this judge does not even fulfill his obligation, but there are too many flaws in this case; they have the means and the power to do exactly what they want to do and there's not a fucking thing you can do about it.

It was asked of the judge if he read the letters of recommendation that were sent by my friends and relatives. He said no he did not and did not know where they were. Someone showed him and then he told the court that he had not have time to read them. (*)

Now here's my life on the line and this judge does not even fulfill his obligation; instead he shirks this obligation.

The next question was asked if he read the report from the parole office, which stated that my sentence should be three years of home confinement because of my ill health. As I recall, he said no, he did not read it nor was he intending to read the report. You can see him getting tired from his big luncheon and was ready to go to sleep, so I, the condemned man, get the short end of his benevolence.

Next was my turn to speak. I give a very eloquent speech, probably on the par of closing statements to that of Perry Mason, but the judge was not even listening to what I had to say. He was like in a fog. I spoke of my illnesses, in particular of my multiple myeloma cancer, which is a disease of the immune system. Multiple myeloma is a rare, very painful and deadly cancer. Regarding my cancer, I went to the state medical school's cancer center in the capitol of my home state for a second opinion and to inquire about clinical trials. After some testing, it was confirmed that I did have the signs of multiple myeloma. I then offered myself to participate in a clinical study but was told at that time there were no studies being conducted.

I attempted to show the judge some of the health records that I brought with me, and of course he was not interested.

Several times during my dissertation, the persecutor pops in and makes some snide remarks or comments that were totally false. This was totally uncalled for and he was out of order and what did the judge do to the prosecutor? Ah, you guessed it? NOTHING!

The judge seemed quite happy to pronounce my sentence. He sentenced me to 48 months, lifetime supervised probation and five years of special counseling, with two days per week of individual sessions and one session per week of group therapy. (*) This, according to others, was an egregious sentence, and I have to explain to you all the nuances and legal abuse that I found out after my release.

It bothers me even today that the judge did not read the letters of recommendation from friends and family or give any credence to the recommendation of the parole office, as they did a lot of work on my case. He also did not work on mens rea as I was promised in court with my first attorney. and it is within the transcript. It is still my contention that he could have sent his secretary to give the verdict, (*) and he could sit back in his office reminiscing about his recent moment of glory at the elongated luncheon, with a well-deserved nap. He made his numbers today, and now as I go to prison you will understand my bitterness. This was no legal trial by any means, but one of a kangaroo court. (*)

One last thing. As I was sentenced I asked him about medical care within the BOP, and he told me bluntly not to worry about the BOP; it has an excellent medical program. Now that's another lie, because I can prove this lie over and over and over again, ad infinitum.

I probably will take the repercussions from my comments, but as I stated before, facts are facts and that is how it was, especially when I still claim my innocence today.

I would've written this book sometime earlier, but I was so ill because of my mistreatment and abuse within the Bureau of Prisons that I was not physically or mentally capable of completing such a task and I will readily admit to you that this possibly is the hardest thing I've ever had to do in my entire life.

People make mistakes.   I do, but I believe I'm a man, human being and I atone for my wrong, but I guess the black robe is a shield preventing responsibility or accountability.

                              It is what it is

My Sentence and Conditions

• • •

Scanned Documents of my Sentence

. . .

page 1 of 7

UNITED STATES DISTRICT COURT

UNITED STATES OF AMERICA
                    Plaintiff
v.

                    Defendant

                                        Defendant's Attorney

JUDGMENT IN A CRIMINAL CASE

THE DEFENDANT pleaded guilty to count(s) 1 of the indictment on

ACCORDINGLY, the court has adjudicated that the defendant is guilty of the following offense(s):

Title, Section & Nature of Offense	Date Offense Ended	Count Number(s)
18:2252(a)(4)(B) POSSESSION WITH INTENT TO VIEW CHILD PORNOGRAPHY		1

The defendant is sentenced as provided in pages 2 through 7 of this judgment. The sentence is imposed pursuant to the Sentencing Reform Act of 1984.

IT IS ORDERED that the defendant must notify the United States Attorney for this district within 30 days of any change of name, residence, or mailing address until all fines, restitution, costs and special assessments imposed by this judgment are fully paid. If ordered to pay restitution, the defendant must notify the court and United States Attorney of any material change in economic circumstances.

Date of Imposition of Judgment

Signature of Judge

Name and Title of Judge

Date

Iam Clarize

IMPRISONMENT

The defendant is hereby committed to the custody of the United States Bureau of Prisons to be imprisoned for a total term of **48 months**.

The Court makes the following recommendations to the Bureau of Prisons.

The defendant is remanded to the custody of the United States Marshal.

RETURN

I have executed this judgment as follows:

Defendant delivered _____ to _____ at _____
_____, with a certified copy of this judgment.

_____
UNITED STATES MARSHAL

By:_____
DEPUTY UNITED STATES MARSHAL

SUPERVISED RELEASE

Upon release from imprisonment, the defendant shall be on a life time supervised release term

The defendant shall report in person to the probation office in the district to which the defendant is released within 72 hours of release from the custody of the Bureau of Prisons.

The defendant shall not commit another federal, state or local crime.

The defendant shall not unlawfully possess a controlled substance. The defendant shall refrain from any unlawful use of a controlled substance.

The defendant shall submit to one drug test within 15 days of release from imprisonment and two (2) periodic drug tests thereafter, as determined by the Court.

The above mandatory drug testing condition is suspended, based on the Court's determination that the defendant poses a low risk of future substance abuse.

The defendant shall not possess a firearm, ammunition, destructive device, or any other dangerous weapon.

The defendant shall cooperate in the collection of DNA as directed by the probation officer.

Iam Clarize

STANDARD CONDITIONS OF SUPERVISION

1. The defendant shall not leave the judicial district without the permission of the Court or probation officer.
2. The defendant shall report to the probation officer in the manner and as frequently as directed by the Court or probation officer.
3. The defendant shall answer truthfully all inquiries by the probation officer and follow the instructions of the probation officer.
4. The defendant shall support his dependents and meet other family responsibilities.
5. The defendant shall work regularly at a lawful occupation unless excused by the probation officer for schooling, training, or other acceptable reasons.
6. The defendant shall notify the probation officer within ten (10) days of any change in residence or employment.
7. The defendant shall refrain from excessive use of alcohol and shall not purchase, possess, use, distribute, or administer any narcotic or other controlled substance, or any paraphernalia related to such substances, except as prescribed by a physician.
8. The defendant shall not frequent places where controlled substances are illegally sold, used, distributed, or administered.
9. The defendant shall not associate with any persons engaged in criminal activity, and shall not associate with any person convicted of a felony unless granted permission to do so by the probation officer.
10. The defendant shall permit a probation officer to visit him or her at any time at home or elsewhere and shall permit confiscation of any contraband observed in plain view by the probation officer.
11. The defendant shall notify the probation officer within seventy-two (72) hours of being arrested or questioned by a law enforcement officer.
12. The defendant shall not enter into any agreement to act as an informer or a special agent of a law enforcement agency without the permission of the Court.
13. As directed by the probation officer, the defendant shall notify third parties of risks that may be occasioned by the defendant's criminal record or personal history or characteristics, and shall permit the probation officer to make such notifications and to confirm the defendant's compliance with such notification requirement.
14. The defendant shall pay the special assessment imposed or adhere to a court-ordered installment schedule for the payment of the special assessment.
15. The defendant shall notify the probation officer of any material change in the defendant's economic circumstances that might affect the defendant's ability to pay any unpaid amount of restitution, fines, or special assessments.

SPECIAL CONDITIONS OF SUPERVISION

The defendant shall participate in sex offender testing and evaluation to include psychological, behavioral assessment and/or polygraph examinations as a means to ensure compliance with program requirements and restrictions. The defendant shall pay all or part of the costs for participation in the program not to exceed the sliding fee scale as established by the Department of Health and Human Services and adopted by this Court.

The defendant shall enter and attend sex-offender-specific group and individual counseling at an approved outpatient treatment program, if warranted from the testing, evaluation and assessments and shall abide by all program requirements and restrictions. The defendant shall pay all or part of the costs for participation in the program not to exceed the sliding fee scale as established by the Department of Health and Human Services and adopted by this Court.

The defendant shall neither possess nor have under his control any matter that is pornographic or that depicts or describes sexually explicit conduct as defined by 18 U.S.C. Section 2256, or any matter depicting sexual activity including any person under the age of eighteen.

The defendant may only have personal access to computer internet services that are approved by the probation officer. The probation officer shall have access to the defendant's personal computer to verify the same.

The defendant shall submit his person, and any property, house, residence, vehicle, papers, computer, other electronic communication or data storage devices or media, and effects, to search at any time, with or without a warrant, by any law enforcement or probation officer with reasonable suspicion concerning a violation of a condition of supervision or unlawful conduct by the defendant.

The defendant shall register with the state sex offender registration agency in the state where the defendant resides, works, or is a student, as directed by the probation officer.

Iam Clarize

CRIMINAL MONETARY PENALTIES

The defendant shall pay the following total criminal monetary penalties in accordance with the schedule of payments set forth in this judgment.

Total Assessment	Total Fine	Total Restitution
$100.00	NONE	NONE

JusXtice ™

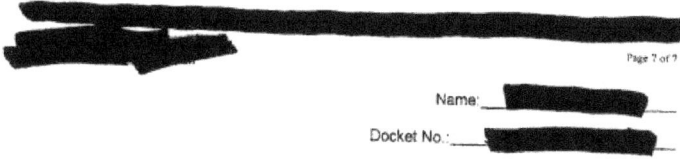

Name: _____

Docket No.: _____

ACKNOWLEDGMENT OF SUPERVISION CONDITIONS

Upon a finding of a violation of probation or supervised release, I understand that the Court may (1) revoke supervision, (2) extend the term of supervision, and/or (3) modify the conditions of supervision.

I have reviewed the Judgment and Commitment Order in my case and the supervision conditions therein. These conditions have been read to me. I fully understand the conditions and have been provided a copy of them.

(Signed)

_____   _____
Defendant   Date

_____   _____
U.S. Probation Officer/Designated Witness   Date

Federal Court Fraternity

• • •

A LOT OF INFORMATION WAS garnered after my release from "the Resort", a name not of endearment, but one of sarcasm and disdain. This is the name, or tag, that I have given to any federal penal institution. An attorney I knew actually coined the name. He is one of the few attorneys that I greatly respected and I am using this name in my respect to him.

I talked to several professionals who know how the system works. Being processed through the system, you will find some things quite enlightening and frightening. By the looks of the courtroom in dark woods, leather chairs, the throne of the judge, the black robe, all giving you the impression of propriety, power and omnipotence designed to make you understand who was in control and who has the power. Like any corporation, of which The United States Government is a corporation, your destiny and fate have already been decided. No matter what you do, nothing will change your predetermined destiny. You may negotiate a little bit, but you are screwed.

The court aesthetics is all part of a well-designed and implemented form of mind control. Yes, I said mind control. A term I am sure they do not want to be known, but the fact remains that there is mind control involved not only within this court system but also within everything that you do under the guise of the Department of injustice. (*) I will discuss this matter of mind control in another chapter or two. I will also discuss other things that you may know little about, and that I did learn after my incarceration through a lot of research.

The external components of this "fraternal" system are just as important as that of the grandiose surroundings of the courtroom, but also what goes on behind the scenes preparing for the push-through of people through the system and to a penal institution as quickly as possible. It is my understanding from others that the judge, prosecutor, and attorneys, all being attorneys, including those paid by the court, that the court would prefer that you use one of their hired hands to plead your case as he would do the bidding of the puppet master.

They have so-called seminars by which there is a gathering of the judges, prosecutors and all attorneys including outside and inside attorneys and probably some of the staff attend a seminar where the rules of the court are dictated and are binding on all participants of that seminar. They have these gatherings which are usually paid for by the Injustice Department. The purpose of these meetings is to conduct speedy trials or in most cases processing a plea bargain. In order to become a member and one of this fraternity, you must abide by its rules, regulations and procedures and policies. And if they do not follow the rules, they will not be allowed into the courtroom to defend the client. Do not attend or disagree and you will not be allowed in the courtroom to defend your client's interest.

It has always been my understanding that the relationship of the court between the defense attorney and the prosecutor is one of an adversarial condition, but now it has turned into something akin to a fraternity.

This is where things have changed and it is no longer an adversarial relationship within the court, but one of paternalism. The original axiom was "you are innocent until proven guilty" has become "you're guilty and must prove your innocence" and if you go to court to profess your innocence and lose, a severe penalty will be assessed to your sentence, usually by a factor of two. This is called stacking and has always been illegal, but practiced by most of the courts and recently the Senate has notified that this law is to be enforced. They are not above the law, but it seems so. When you look around at what's happening today, well, you can put two and two together. I'm sure the courts are no different. This is an illegal practice called stacking where the judge can impose a sentence that is two or three times the amount dictated by the sentencing guidelines. It is my contention that my sentence was stacked. (*) But the findings and rulings of the Senate came after my sentence and I cannot do anything about it, and even if the law is broken, nothing will be done about it. It all depends on who you are and your relationship to the laws and punishments. It is not unusual for the court to make up their own rulings to assist them in persecuting another victim going to jail.

At the state level, I have learned that the success ratio of the state convictions is about 50 to 60%. At least the person has a chance, and if they lose, the state usually does not stack additional time onto the sentence.

Just recently Congress has passed a law to quell the abuse regarding stacking. It was against the law to stack sentences irrelevant to the case for additional time, but was used on a wide basis throughout the country. Congress had to come back in and tell them to obey the law. Those who are supposed to uphold the law often abuse the law. My sentence was stacked. (*)

Another case in point: Congress has passed a law stating that a certain percentage of a person's time be allocated for good time, and if the person served the sentence, well, he has earned good time as a reduction of time at the end of the sentence. I believe the figure was 10% but I don't want to be quoted. The Bureau of Prisons (BOP) made up their own percentage which retains the end date for an additional amount of time, violating the law that Congress has passed for them to abide. (*) How do I know this? Because I was involved in this calculation and they could never tell me how they calculated this number that they came up with while it was a simple percentage of the sentence that was given at the trial. Also, it was in some of the trade magazines that I read that brought this noncompliance with the law to the forefront. The BOP made you stay in their grip for a longer period of time probably to extract more monies from the taxpayers. (*)

The point is that there are two sets of rules, one made by Congress and the other rules or policies made by the Department of Justice for their own specific needs and to hell with the Congress.

Now it is at the forefront today and shows that there are two different classes of individuals within the country. One contains 99.5% ordinary citizens and the others may be classified in a privileged class, who are above the law. (*) While incarcerated I met many attorneys, doctors, lawyers, politicians, senators and many others who fall into this normal category, but others like Hillary Clinton trample all over the Constitution with newly sharpened nails on their track shoes as they stomp. She's not the only one, there are others but with the elitist group.

Did you notice the word "slave"? I have now become a slave to the United States government by the 13th amendment to the Constitution of the United States. More on this subject of governmental slaves and mind control in other chapters. These are some little-known factoids that I found through my research and would like to share them with you. (*)

I was quite surprised to see how openly this fraternity situation exists. However, very few that we have found will do any work or represent any client within the federal structure. So, if you get in trouble in this area, you will have trouble finding an attorney to represent you, if you need one, because I feel you're going to plead guilty anyway. You have little or no choice. There is a saying that I learned in prison that is applicable to the situation and others, and you will hear it over and over again, "It is what it is." I know that is bad grammar, but it is what it is.

It is what it is

Overzealous Prosecutor

• • •

Many articles that I have read in my research now speak of how the prosecutors, or persecutors as I like to call them, now seem to control the courts and the judge is only to announce the decision as created by the persecutor.

In most of the districts, the persecutor makes far more money than the judge. This just goes to show who now runs the court system.

I feel there is a complete disconnect with the Constitution of The United States and it recognizes an adversarial situation so that the defendant is somewhat about a voice or a means of fighting the claims as set before him. But we all know, today that is, it's just the opposite as a court now has full control of the future of the defendant, guilty or not, and the persecutor is now conferring with the judge on the defendant's punishment.

The system started back in the HW Bush era when he allegedly announced that those who are in jail can rot in jail. This is probably the most disgusting thing I've ever heard from a president. Also my current readings on this president have been less than stellar and his stupid thousand points of light are nothing more than silver dollars in his pocket. I have read how he came to power and one organization that brought him fame and fortune started with Yale's Skull and Bones. But he is not alone; there are many others. Therefore, I have put in the appendix several books to read regarding the Committee of 300.

Each person should be looked at as an individual and his sentencing should be imposed in accordance with his background, his state of mind and even the possibility or potential of his doing further harm once he is released. This should be taken on a case-by-case basis and not by sentencing guidelines put together by five or six people who think they are God. I spoke about this in detail in another chapter and rather than raise my blood pressure up to a high level, please read about that section.

Thank you for letting my blood stay in my vessels.
It is what it is

Out of my Element

• • •

How would you feel jumping into a **15-feet-deep pool** and not knowing how to swim? How would you feel going down the world's largest roller coaster for the first time? How would you feel if somebody is pointing a gun at you? How would you feel being a passenger in a car with someone driving at breakneck speeds and drunk? These are all temporary fears you would encounter in the situations, but now it's been these fears for days, months and even years. Would you not change in any fashion? Or are you fearless? I really doubt that you are fearless. I was not.

I was trying to explain the feeling of helplessness, fear, being out of place in another world in which you have no control, and all these others that surround you are NOT YOUR FRIENDS. (*) Each of these that surround you has one job to do, except for one. The one person who was supposed to be your ally, friend, mentor and your fighter for your rights, and that was your attorney. But if your attorney happens to side with the others in the room, you're naked in the wilderness, as there is no one there to assist you, as all of the others now have one goal, **SEND YOU TO JAIL** for as long as they can and sometimes even further. (*)

You are out of your element. I was out of my element and there is no hope, there is no real justice, only despair, because your ass is grass and they are the big lawnmower.

It is tough enough to have a good attorney, but they are held by the rules of the court, which handcuffed them and there is no longer this adversarial role that the Constitution of the United States proclaims. There is no longer the mantra of "you are innocent until proven guilty." Scrub your mind of that saying, because it has no worth in today's world. The system is so skewed that they are assured victory 98.6% of the time. And if you should go to trial and win, you're free to go. But if you lose, there is a penalty of doubling your sentence, called stacking, (*) which is illegal. Stacking will be discussed in another chapter.

I did not have a chance even though I was innocent, **and not able to prove my innocence,** but my attorney told me that he would not defend me because he said that the persecutor was too strong for him and that he would lose, thereby they would double my sentence.

What chance does one have when you're not even dealt a hand that you could even pick up, but you pay your dues and you lose every single time.

President Trump stated that the Justice Department is screwed up and he is so correct. (*)

When this book is published, I will have an envelope ready to accept the book and send it on to President Trump. I will also be sending it to other areas.

I am not writing this book really for myself or for profit, because the rest of my life has been ruined and I have no possible recourse for me and my wife's safety for the rest of my life. I received a particularly harsh sentence. **Others who have committed the**

crime and even more heinous than I and they were given lenient sentences as compared to mine. I ask you why? I asked them why? I ask everyone why? And I have yet to receive an answer from anyone. (*) Many of those in the know say that I have been screwed.

So, I will go on writing. The only thing that could stop me from writing would be that the Justice Department would pick me up and put me away so that no one will ever find me again. And I know for a fact that this is done. I do not joke about this fact, as it is real.

Now I say unto you, my dear readers, protect yourselves that the laws are changing and now even the most minimal amount of a crime is becoming federal, such as spousal beating and drunk driving. (*)

The United States used to have the judicial system that was the envy of the world, but today, I will not tell you what is thought about the current judicial system. Go on the Internet and find out for yourself. The answers are there.

It is what it is

What Happens in the Courts Today

• • •

THE COURT SYSTEM SET UP by our founding fathers was one of an adversarial nature. In other words, one side, the prosecution, is to be in contention with the defense, and the defense has full right to all the evidence that is gathered by the persecutor and he is to strongly defend his client. I guess my attorney just didn't attend those sessions while he was in "law" school. I was going to make a comment here about my "wonderful" attorney; he's not worth the effort. By the by, I have not time to any of these individual since leaving the resort, nor do I intend to. I have more productive things to do and since the writing of this book I have enough work to last me for the next three or four years working a minimum of 10 hours a day seven days a week.

The judge keeps pomp and circumstance of a fair trial, for the defendant is guided that this is going to be a quick and fair trial. It is on this basis that our country has lived for centuries but within the last 30 to 40 years things have changed drastically where the persecutor is not only the persecutor but also takes the role of the judge and actually tells the judge and controls the judge into making a decision in his favor or close to his recommendations, and in most cases, threatens the defendants with extended jail terms if they should happen to lose at trial. (*)

You will probably hear a lot of people within the judicial system state that my comments are false and out of order. But I lived within the prison system for a number of years and talked to many inmates and in talking with them I got the same story and mine is a synopsis of what they all said. I have found inmates, with the rudimentary library and information, who know how quite well how to investigate and build a case. And there are a lot of cases won by these jailhouse lawyers. In fact, one is a friend of mine who wins a high percentage of cases for other individuals. And he is one of the nicest individuals I have ever met. He always has a kind word, always. In my sorrow for him, is that he's going to be in there for a while, after I leave. But he will continue his work. God bless him.

With their techniques, pressures and innuendos I was eventually forced into a plea bargain. And if I knew beforehand what I know today, I would not put up with the garbage. I have one other alternative which I did not take and that I am sorry today I did not do because I do believe I would be a free man today. And that is I should have gone pro se. (*) I know I can do much better than my attorneys have done, especially the last one, who was simply awful.

I know of one man, a doctor, who paid an attorney $250,000 to represent him and all he got was a little better time off of his original sentence as he had to take a plea bargain. You will see how this works later in this book. There is no way you win in the judicial system today, as it is designed and devised so that anyone who has that mishap of being in the FBI's sites is destined for a penal institution of the BOP, and for many it is a death sentence.

So that mantra or the model as established with our founders being "you are innocent until proven guilty" has now been changed to a corrected version of what actually happens: you are guilty; now prove your innocence. (*)

The cards are stacked against you no matter what you do and if you are caught and are charged with a crime, I feel so sorry for you.

I know of an Indian that I met while incarcerated who worked on the cars of these drug people. The drug leader of this gang turned on him, so that he could get a lesser sentence, but this poor guy never did drugs, or sold drugs in any shape or form, nor was he involved with drugs, but was sent to prison for three years just for working on their cars.

You think this is egregious? I would hope so; the way things are going it is going to get worse.

I know of another inmate who is a doctor, or I should say a doctor that can no longer practice medicine except in very special circumstances. His claim, and I do believe him, was that he had evidence to prove his innocence in a building he owned and he claims that the FBI burned it down, so that this evidence would never show up in court. His practice was very successful and he practiced within the ghetto of a city. He told me how he did it, and such a wise man he was. He was very successful and made a lot of money and that maybe triggered the FBI, but I do not know. He told me how he made his money, as he was a doctor in the ghetto of a large city, but he built a mall-like affair with many businesses that were associated with this practice. He had beauty shops, restaurants and other businesses that his patients used while waiting for his attention. He was one very shrewd businessman and an excellent doctor. I got to know him quite well and I'm sorry I won't be able to visit with him anytime in the future. The interesting thing about our relationship was that he pushed me around in my wheelchair and to this day I am extremely grateful for his friendship and his assistance.

I have met with senators, Catholic priests, all kinds of religious people, singers, music award winners, all types and sorts of people I have met. I will admit to you that probably a good 95+% plus are guilty, but there are a few that are not guilty as charged.

There are many similar stories throughout the penal institution and I could tell you a few more where many of these inmates have been done wrong.

I pray that one of these days everybody will get a fair chance, at least a chance in the justice system, but now everyone is doomed. If you are called into court for any infraction of the federal law, just go and kiss your ass goodbye. It makes no matter what circumstance you have; it is over, but I feel so sorry for you because your life has now been changed for the worse. (*)

I will be talking a lot more about the subjects and a lot more about my stay at the resort in my second book. If you thought this one might be a little bit interesting, the next one will far surpass this one. It will be a most enjoyable read
                        It is what it is

Mens Rae

• • •

Mens rea in criminal law is viewed as one of the necessary elements of some crimes. The standard common law test of criminal liability is usually expressed in the Latin phrase, actus reus non facit reum nisi mens sit rea, which means "the act is not culpable unless the mind is guilty".

This law has been interpreted by legal scholars and assesses the age, health and previous convictions or conflicts with the law when the person is charged with the crime. In other words, a person's history is an indication of his aptitude to commit crime, except for maybe a parking or speeding ticket. I was 69 years old, in poor health, with no run-ins or conflicts with the law. To be succinct, I was a virgin to crime. I was always a law-abiding citizen.

It is within the court records that; <u>the trial judge stated that he would personally look into Mens Rae as pertaining to my case</u>. I don't know what happened to the judge, but I think he is suffering from dementia and/or he suddenly became prejudicial against me. I believe the latter is the strongest possibility.

I was going before the magistrate court regarding my plea bargain and I talked to both persecutor and my dumb ass attorney wondering if I was going to jail after this event and they told me no, that was not in the plan, and I told them I wanted this in writing before venturing into this meeting. The document was signed prior to the meeting and all did not go well because this magistrate displayed a pompous attitude sitting on his high throne and glaring down at his diminutive subjects below him. I guess, I was destined to go to jail but with this contract, he had to relinquish and he was very angry. And I hear from my so-called attorney that he and the persecutor were admonished for their actions by the judge as I was supposed to go to jail that day and spend the rest of my time in solitary confinement until my trial and sentencing. I'm also guessing that the judge got his ass reamed by the Circuit Court. From this I think the judge and persecutor turned very prejudicial and were ready to bury my ass, and I believe that is why I am now serving what may be akin to a death sentence, that I never will leave the grasp of the DOI.

Because I served the unjust sentence and have parole for the rest of my life, which is really akin to being in a prison without bars and also the most egregious part of this entire circumstance is that I have become a SLAVE of the United States Government according to the 13th Amendment of the Constitution of the United States.

There is a story about this magistrate that I must tell you. This will give an insight as to his character and being such a true story. At one time, I was a gym rat and worked out in the gym four days a week. I lost weight and bulked up at one time and was able to flex my pecks as bodybuilders do. I was quite proud of this very difficult achievement. This magistrate for a period of time came to the gym and worked out at the same time that I did. This gym is basically for businessmen, attorneys and professionals. Not that others can't join or to work out, but it was just that type of gym. It is rather friendly and everybody greets each other by their first name. Except for this magistrate as he has thrown some temper tantrums for anyone calling him by his first name and we were to address him as "your honor". That's right, we were in the gym and we had to address him as your honor. Not me, I was not going to get anywhere close to that pompous, well you know what I mean.

I digress... The bottom line is that I think the judge never looked into mens rea in regards to my case, but rather ignored it because he was chewed out by the District Court. Therefore, I was denied my legal right for this law. It was known that certain individuals are above the law, and you will see more of this as we go on, and as you are seeing now with the conflict at hand.

It is the opinion of many others that with my background in the way the sentencing guidelines are written for this particular offense, I should never have been accused of that offense in the first place and that my penalty was far and above any other similar crimes committed and even worse crimes receive lesser sentences. In other words, I was abused, retaliated against and persecuted.

Be cautious dear readers, of the long arm and the short arm of the law, because my readings and research have shown me that all of us are at any time in violation of the laws three or four times a day.

There is an excellent book that I have read that discusses this issue in detail:

THREE FELONIES A DAY
HOW THE FEDS TARGET THE INNOCENT
by: Harvey A Silverglate

The number of laws have skyrocketed since 1985, and you are supposed to know each law. It is told that even attorneys coming out of law school cannot comprehend the magnitude and weight of not only the meaning of the laws, but the multitude of them. If you try to look for them you can't find them because there is no repository that holds these laws for your viewing. I have tried to find these and I cannot and with all the breadth of knowledge that is based upon the Internet, these laws are not available to the public for your knowledge. So you, like I am, are SCREWED. And if you get into trouble and have to go before the court and have a very prejudicial judge persecutor and a kowtowing attorney, your destiny is doomed.

Suffice it to say, I did not stand a chance, nor will you.

An official within the Justice Department referred to the fact that I was charged, sentenced and convicted for what I MIGHT do.

Others who are within the judicial system have told me that I have been screwed. They were dead set against getting me into prison for some extended period of time so as to fulfill their mantra, which is to get individuals into the system for the reasons of MONEY.

I am not a legal scholar, but a little common sense can tell you that something is very wrong. I was unjustly and forcibly mandated to commit myself to a life of hell for the rest of my life. Because to attain the status that I have is nothing more than a living death sentence of which I have no end and which mandates strict restrictions on everything that I do. I have no life. The only life I have is with my wife of 50 years and a few close friends and two of my three brothers.

I need to tell you again that I am a 73-year-old white male who was arrested when I was 69 years old and the only crimes that I have committed were speeding and parking tickets. I've always lived within the guidelines of the law, as far as I know.

There are so many laws these days that we do not know if an innocuous crime has been committed as there are too many laws for us to know about and they do not have a repository where we can find out and what laws exist today keep multiplying. I also was suffering from a multitude of health issues and was diagnosed with multiple myeloma which is a painful, rare and deadly cancer of the blood. I shall fight, against all odds, to live a long-lasting life, even though I am a slave.

It is what it is

Discovery

• • •

DEFINITION OF DISCOVERY:
DISCOVERY, IN THE LAW OF the United States and other countries, is a pre-trial procedure in a lawsuit in which each party, through the law of civil procedure, can obtain evidence from the other party or parties by means of discovery devices such as a request for answers to interrogatories, request for production of documents, request for admissions and depositions. Discovery can be obtained from non-parties using subpoenas. When a discovery request is objected to, the requesting party may seek the assistance of the court by filing a motion to compel discovery.

My Supposed Discovery
In the first place, I was not aware that I could petition the court for discovery, because my attorney tells me nothing. I asked several times of my attorney for discovery, and each time he negated my request. In all fact, he told me that he and the "persecutor" (federal prosecutor) went to the main FBI office within the state and there they said they saw the evidence against me. (*)

This point that deeply concerns me is that they drove together for two and half hours one way in the same vehicle and had a chance to discuss my case and how they were going to screw me as they so judiciously have done. (*)

My attorney says I was not to worry about it because he would be able to work with the "persecutor" on having a very decent plea agreement, which was quite the opposite of what actually happened and I received the harshest sentence not only for jail time, but also for parole. I have a lifetime of parole, which is tantamount to incarceration on the outside, a literal death sentence. I'm always under the thumb of my parole officer, who by the way is very nice to me and I feel the parole office knows, I am sure, that I have been screwed, blued and tattooed. Also, I obey the rules set forth to me and I do not cause problems. In my case it is tantamount to home confinement.

I knew from the original indictment that things were awry, because the indictment names some of the files and extensions of these images that were to condemn me. One of these file extensions has to do with peer to peer relationships, in other words I can use your computer you can use mine for storage and use of computer time. This was done at the time when hard drives were not large enough to store the music and videos prominent in the day for college students. Today, the hard drives are huge for data storage and file sharing programs are no longer necessary, and now the cloud can store your pictures, files or whatever you wish. These file sharing techniques were used on college campuses and at times caused the main computers on a campus to crash.

If I had this information I know that I could have dispelled the items that I was supposed to be associated with. I was not allowed to bring forward anything. I literally was unable to defend myself. (*) My attorney did me a great disservice, but this is not the only place by which he is responsible for my eventual incarceration and lifetime death sentence.

I was incarcerated and there was nothing I could do to help myself with the situation. I was condemned by my malicious adversaries of the "DOI" (Department of Injustice). But my wife contracted with an attorney who employed another attorney who knew the ins and outs and byways of the federal court system and he went in and he <u>*looked into my records to find that* **DISCOVERY WAS NEVER MADE.**</u> (*) This was a vehement disregard for my rights, and the court system under which I was tried got away with it and they got away with a lot more. Every time I think about these facts I get depressed, and writing about this causes me great depression, but I must push through so that you will be able to read my trials and tribulations.

I have been so wronged, did not have a chance to even defend myself. I know today what I should've done.

<u>What I Should Have Done</u> (*)

- got rid of my attorney and gone pro se
- demanded discovery
- learned more about what is going on and hopefully I could find something about stacking
- know not to trust anyone; they are not trying to help you, they are trying to incarcerate you, that is their job
- fight and scratch tooth and nail, assume that you are going to jail but go as a man or woman, and not like a wimp like I

- remember something, each time a person is sent to incarceration, it is the death sentence - not necessarily death in the physical sense, which it can be, but by death socially, economically, physically, psychologically all wrapped up into one nice little ball

You have to fight, no one will do it for you.
$\quad\quad\quad\quad\quad\quad\quad\quad$ It is what it is

Stacking

• • •

I LEARNED THE TERM STACKING while I was within "the resort" to mean that additional sentencing time can be added to your original indictment at the will and whim of the court. There may be other names for this procedure, but this is the term I have learned and use. I personally believe it is very abusive, cruel and very unnecessary.

This to me is one of the most egregious forms of punishment within the Department of injustice. In simple terms, it is adding onto a person sentence outside of the parameters that have been set up by the Congress of the United States.

Stacking always had been an illegal procedure within the judicial system but over a period of time this illegal procedure was slowly implemented and became the norm of the day. Many have suffered from the consequences of this illegal device and have spent many additional years imprisoned when they should have been released.

At some time when I was imprisoned I found out that Congress caught the judicial department in an illegal action and came down on them to change their ways to what Congress has told them to do. But it seems the judicial system always likes to make some of their own rules. Now they have to abide by the rules of Congress.

I was a victim of this illegal action and discovered additional time, how much time I don't know but from what I do know, my initial number of images REPORTED BY THE COMPUTER COMPANY TO WHICH I TOOK MY COMPUTER FOR REPAIR was relatively low, generally speaking. They were not my images, but I am using this as an example. Somehow, they brought the number up to being possibly in the thousands as I really don't know. Also, it is illegal to comp the same image more than once. Now do you think they would do such a thing? Rest assured that they would and they do. (*)

It is what it is

Intended and Unintended Consequences

• • •

WHENEVER ANY DECISION IS MADE there are always consequences which have a great bearing upon the effectiveness or the original intent of policy or law that was created. When any policy or law was created, many times due diligence is only an afterthought when the unintended becomes a nightmare reality.

There are unintended consequences that are not foreseen at the time the decision or policy becomes effective. These unintended consequences can and will have a positive, negative or neutral effect upon the decision or created policy. It is usually the unintended consequences that wreak havoc on what the original intent was to achieve and have deleterious effects on the policy, creating a monster.

It is the recipient of the policy or decision that suffers the adverse effect and can and does cause a lot more problems overshadowing what the positive original intent was to create a larger and unchangeable problem.

In my case with the judicial system, the policies or decisions that were made that affected my outcome, I do not believe are unintended consequences, but the deliberate actions and decisions were made either as prejudicial, spiteful or just being a plain super-aggressive methodology to meet a demand created to keep the federal prisons full of new inmates at whatever cost. Again, the resulting methodology is MONEY.

It is my contention and belief that the judicial department set forth its strategy to give me a maximum jail time with full knowledge and intent at any cost.

I do believe that I am not the only one who has suffered in this horrible matter. The entire group, the judge, the persecutor, the magistrate and my supposed attorney planned my outcome far in advance of my actual sentencing date. In other words, I was doomed, screwed and tattooed at the very beginning, but they had to put on the dog and pony show. I never stood a chance because of the predisposition of the court. (*)

I do believe that there was a prejudiced factor against me. One factor I believe and question is why they were inclined to lie or make up things to justify a predisposed decision that was unilaterally made. They are making or bending the rules to suit their specific needs and to hell with the law and also its victim, me. (*)

I fully believe I was prejudiced against, and this prejudicial action will be discussed in a chapter unto itself.

Many laws that have been made and are such that the unintended consequences are not observed, therefore, creating a major problem, and rectification is not possible.

It is what it is

Attorney Says No Trial

• • •

I HAD THREE ATTORNEYS. ONE was fired, another one quit because I felt he was not representing me and he didn't like being told what to do. We were paying for his services and he got the judge involved; the judge was displeased with me as I wrote him a letter, so I fired the attorney.

A serious mistake I made is the court appointed an attorney for me who was one sorry incompetent individual. The best thing I could've done in this case would've been to go pro se, but you do not know about these things or think of it when you're under this type of stress as there are many people against you and you are only one. The law is in their favor, and they can do anything they want to you as they can make things up and change things around and sometimes not even tell the full truth, the whole truth, and nothing but the truth, but by God if you mess up in the process you are in for extended jail time. There is a no-win situation for you and me within this current judicial system.

When I visited the court-appointed attorney, he talked mostly about his one great escapade of how he got great plea bargains for his clients, one a notorious drug dealer. I wondered if he ever won a case. I thought that he was rather strange. When I spoke to him he was more concerned about the money he was receiving and how to pay for his children's tuition as they were going to a private Catholic school. I would hear of more of his problems and his one success with one drug dealer out of Chicago on a plea bargain.

I kept asking him about discovery and he told me not to worry about it because he and the persecutor (prosecutor) went to the state capital to the FBI Office and looked at the evidence. I never saw the evidence. He said that they observed and planned to work things out together and I was not to worry. I was mistaken as I jumped hook line and sinker into the lion's mouth for listening to him.

We did find out later through another attorney who investigated my case after I was incarcerated that there was never discovery made. This is egregious. I asked for discovery and never received it and I was entitled to it.

My Attorney Screwed me and Lied to me. (*) (*)

If I saw the discovery I would know what is the problem.

A couple of weeks before I was to get involved with the plea bargain, my court-appointed attorney came out and told me that he would not defend me in a court trial as the "persecutor" (prosecutor) is too strong for him and is too tough in these cases and that he would not be able to win because the "persecutor" controls the jury to do his bidding and my only chance was a plea bargain. This is the time when I should've gone pro se. Mistake number 1 was a big error in my case, but no one is of sound mind under these conditions. If I had known what I know today, I really believe I would have walked out of there a free man, because they had no case against me; it was all BULLSHIT. (*)

He also told me that if I went to trial and if I won the case, I would walk free, however if I lost the case, they would double the sentence. This is called stacking in legal terminology. (*)

Stacking is when additional time is added to your sentence for any reason that can be contrived by the court. In the past, it had been illegal to stack additional time onto a sentence for any reason, but it became a common practice until Congress found out about it and put a stop to this nefarious illegal action, but my trial was during the time that the illegal action was "sanctioned ", so therefore I do not qualify for any vindication. I have no recourse; that is totally BULLSHIT. Here I sit struggling for my health, I had a sentence that was unjustly placed, my attorney did not do anything about it because he is inept, he bootlicked the persecutor and probably is afraid of his own shadow.

Now can you believe this? The night before the trial my wife and I were in his office and he tells us what he felt the outcome would be. The probation department had suggested a three-year probation term because of my health. Also, I would be on home confinement for the period of time. Even today, this bothers me a lot. But I'm not finished yet.

It is around 5 o'clock and he tells us that he has to go home and play with kids and fix dinner then write the closing remarks for the next day. I was sick. I was in disbelief to think he had not even written his closing remarks for something that was going to determine this outcome of my life. This is sheer incompetence at the highest level and even to make to this is just plain stupid.

My wife was in contact with him after the trial for something regarding my sentencing, but he refused help, apparently because he would not receive payment. But it is my understanding that the court was still paying him as my attorney. Needless we are very disappointed in this attorney's counsel.

Sometimes you have to do things for yourself and even if the odds are far against you, you have to try, while in my case I turned to be a wimp and I am mad at myself to this day. I've always been a fighter, I really didn't hear anyone or anything, but the number of people against you in an arena that you know nothing about, and I turned into a wimp, as I was. BUT NOT ANYMORE!

I have been in many battles in business, but there were rules. They were tough ones, but they worked. In this case, I was a neophyte, a novice, a dreamer, but I believed in my heart of hearts that the Justice Department was fair, but to my amazement they are quite the contrary.

So, I advise you my dear readers, if you are ever caught in a situation where you deal with any of the personnel within the Justice Department be prepared, learn all you can, understand that they are in a brotherhood, and if possible find a decent attorney, if you can.

It is what it is

Interstate and Intrastate Commerce Informaton

• • •

Interstate commerce, in U.S. constitutional law: any commercial transactions or traffic that crosses state boundaries or that involve more than one state. The traditional concept that the free flow of commerce between states should not be impeded has been used to affect a wide range of regulations, both federal and state. Interstate commerce crosses state lines and is within the federal government's authority to regulate if it chooses.

Intrastate commerce is conducted within a state's borders - state law applies, unless a preemptive federal law applies.

Commerce is the activity of buying and selling of goods and services, especially on a large scale. The system includes legal, economic, political, social, cultural and technological systems that are in operation in any country or internationally.

I HAVE HEARD IT SAID that the definition of interstate and intrastate commerce is changing within the law. It appears that the federal government wants more control over goods and services crossing borders of the states. It states however on the other hand what goods and services going to other states because that brings it monies to that state in the form of taxation. The states also want their autonomy and freedom from the federal government's many demands.

As far as I know at this writing, the rules and regulations have not changed and that the old way of doing business remain sovereign within the state.

For commerce to take place there must be a "meeting of the minds" between the parties. This is basic law 101.

" BOTH PARTIES" agree for commerce or business to happen. There must be some form or some type of agreement for this is to happen. An example would be over the Internet. I buy something from Amazon, they ship it to me and I receive it and vice versa. I give them the credit card number and they bill me for the items received. This is commerce, whether it be within the state, or across state lines. We did not talk to each other about the transaction, but it is a known quantity that I am buying with money and the product will be shipped to me and I can accept it or return the item. This is commerce.

There must be something of some type of value on each side of this equation, or a tit-for-tat. If the item is only one-sided, such as a person captures a picture on the Internet that he would like to have, and there's no safeguard against its being copied, this is a one-sided event. There is no commerce. This may be called theft, or a gift by an unknown source, but there is no commerce. The grantee of this picture is allowing others to copy the picture without any stipulations. This is not commerce. There is no quid pro quo, (or one thing for another) for something of some type of value is exchanged. That is allowing others to have what is placed as if it is a gift. There are no strings attached with this supposed transaction.

In my case, I was forced to lie. Yes, I was forced to lie because they told me if I did not agree that intra-interstate commerce was involved my sentence would increase, or I would get stacked, which is an illegal action. (*)

I argued with the judge, who quickly silenced me with punishment and said that I must attest to that I committed illegal commerce, but there was no commerce. So, under his direction, I lied, and I am not proud of this even to this day. He had all the power and I was just a slave to the Master's commands. (*)

I was never involved in any type of commerce as they stipulated, because I did nothing wrong. I was in contact with no one, nor did I even know of anyone who had such images. I do belong to a couple of forums, but these were all work-related and had to do with my website and how to make it to grow. My emails were almost exclusively for business and a few with my close friends. All my telephone calls were business related. All these things can be checked and verified, but they had no proof of any kind that I was participating in the illegal interstate and intrastate commerce. And yet, I was forced to lie in court, under fuming demands of the judge and the persecutor. This action is called perjury, which is illegal, especially within the federal court. Now I am in a dilemma. I just confessed to perjury, but I was held under extreme duress, while on the other hand, I am innocent of the charges brought before me. What a conundrum. The innocent is forced under duress to commit illegal actions.

It is off to jail I go, again, unless the statute of limitations has been exhausted.

Now you can visualize, where the court can do whatever it pleases, legal or illegal, to accomplish their goals. They do not have any accountability. They rule with complete autonomy and are unto themselves omnipotent, all-powerful, all wise, untouchable, almighty and cannot do wrong, because they lack accountability. This is true of the court that I was in but I am confident that there is a lot of subversion within the courts.

So, my dear readers, I again caution you as you may have to do things that you never thought that you would have to do while you're under the "protection of the court" **to go** against your moral and ethical standards.

After all my experiences within this court system I have changed my thoughts and ethnicity forever because I am now cynical, wary and ever watchful instead of seeing the court as my friend and protector. Now I fear their retaliation. If that is to be, SO BE IT. (*)

                It is what it is

The Big Lie Made Under Severe Duress

• • •

I was in the court to face the judge and the prosecutor along with my incompetent attorney, and that's being nice. They asked me questions regarding my plea bargain, which was a farce as many of the items were not germane to my case. I don't know why they had so many different accusations and innuendos as I had nothing to say in the whole matter as I had to accept what I was given which is akin to a living death sentence. I now associate myself with the living dead and also of being a slave to the United States government. More on this later.

There is one particular part of this ordeal that plagues me today. There was a part in the plea bargain that said something about my being involved in intrastate and interstate commerce. This is total BULLSHIT. I was never involved in any kind of commerce and having to admit under duress was a big fat lie.

First let me explain this to you as I understand it, and if anyone has a different interpretation, they need to revisit the meanings.

Commerce is giving goods or services to an individual or company in exchange for other goods and services. It could be as simple as my giving you five baseball cards that I got in a bubblegum wrapper in exchange for a giant pearl marble. Yes, I used to collect baseball cards and I played marbles when I was young and in grade school, which may be far beyond your years of experience. We did not have cell phones or other niceties that you all have today. Your parents may have stated that they had walked long distances or had to catch a bus to go to school. I was no different. I know that things are different today, but some things remain the same as they were in the past and trading marbles for bubblegum cards was commerce then and it is commerce today.

For commerce to exist there must be a meeting of the minds in some fashion, in that one party is in receipt of some goods or services while the other is exchanging another type of goods or services and then the cycle of commerce is now complete. There is a relationship between the two parties.

In my case, there was no exchange of any goods or services, therefore commerce did not exist. I was not involved in this arena. I did not communicate with anyone via the Internet, telephone, email, regular mail, Internet forums or pay any monies for any goods such as images to be viewed at my pleasure. I had nothing to view, and no goods or services to supply, so therefore I was not involved in interstate or intrastate commerce. But the judge in all his magnificence hounded me to admit that I was involved in interstate and intrastate commerce, which was a bold based lie, and I knew it. But then again, he is a perpetrator of this lie, and I was just an innocent subject for his brutal domination.

When asked this question for me to affirm the statement, I denied that I was involved in interstate or intrastate commerce. The judge and persecutor became livid and angry at me and told me that I attested to this back in an earlier court session and I said

I did not, at which time he threatened me and promised me that I will receive a harsher sentence as I have already pleaded guilty to a crime I did not commit and had to plead out. I think you're getting the gist of how cruel they really are.

Since I was in this courtroom earlier regarding this matter and the judge was certainly against me as well as the persecutor and my inept attorney were all gaping at me to answer the question to their liking or else there will be a hanging in town tonight and I will be the hangee.

So, what do I do, I committed perjury. Yes, I committed perjury and could receive more punishment because of my actions, but no, they just wanted my perjured answer so that they can hang me in another matter.

This bothers me today and it will for the rest of my life that I had to lie in court. I do not like to lie and I do not, because there is no need to; the truth always wins. If I've done something wrong or is that something I should have not, I will tell the truth and suffer the consequences of my actions as I have done many times in the past. At times the consequences could be deleterious to my being, but I would feel much better about it in the end. I was at the start of my life as I slide into the abyss of my current mental health problems. These problems grow as the abuse intensifies during my stay within the judicial system which includes the BOP.

I think I'm finally going to get some help, I do pray to God.
It is what it is

Legal Blackmail

• • •

I CANNOT BELIEVE WHAT HAPPENED to me and the circumstances are quite unusual and I believe illegal. About two to three weeks before my sentencing, I was called into court about a particular matter. The court received a letter from an attorney in another state that claimed that his client, a child, was abused and filmed by a man. He claimed that I had a copy of this film, therefore, I was guilty as a person abusing this child in making a film. I was advised by the judge, that they could fight this case, but I had better gather the money as they negotiated $1000 fee to make this case go away. The original settlement was for $2500. The court supposedly checked with the FBI and this child was not one of the individuals supposedly contained on my hard drive. Gosh, I wonder why not? Could it be that the hard drive did not contain many or any images?

The judge was vehement in my getting the thousand dollars on a certified check to him within two days, or more serious ramifications will be taken against me.

To my mind this is nothing but a scam by an attorney who can't make any money, so he finds a poor child that has been abused and checks all the records in all states to define a possible connection to her terrible past and files suit against that person and takes probably a healthy proportion of the scavenged money for himself. This is what I call legal blackmail.

Why did I roll over because of the judge's feat and will do what he said to do, I do not know? But, each day I curse myself being part of this blackmail. That was wrong. I was a sucker, and I fell for their plan, as I never really knew who received the money. What is the game to get money out of me?

It was sometime after the fact that I realized that I have been legally blackmailed and I felt like throwing up. I have been hoodwinked and bamboozled and there was not a damn thing I could do about it. It was a win for them and a loss for me, again. (*)

I find it amazing that the court can make you do anything against your will. I find that they have so much power that no human should control. There are no checks and balances or accountability within this little group. They run autonomous with no regard for anyone except themselves. Do you not think they are a bit selfish?

Here is just another way how the general public gets SCREWED. (*) Not only do you deal with the current justice system that is going to incarcerate you, but from so-called attorneys trying to collect money in a devious manner. I guess I would not have too much objection if I had to pay money for something I did, but to pay $1000 for something I did not do is far beyond anything that I could call JUSTICE. I firmly believe that this attorney is a blackmailer and a scoundrel. (*)

Another thought came to my mind as I was just getting ready to close this chapter. Could my persecutors be also involved in this scam or sham? The little I know, just a thought. (*)

It is what it is

My Assessment

• • •

SOME, BUT THEN AGAIN MANY, may say that this is just another life experience, but I beg to differ with them as at my age I don't need to go through another hell as I've had enough grief in my life.

I have been put through hell. I have been abused, mistreated, persecuted, retaliated against and victimized by the country I so dearly love. One would think I would be mad at my country, but I am not. I know, and many others know, that there are major problems within this country with the elitists who are trying to take it over and are working towards one world government, and these are the offenders to this great country and they need to be set aside, sequestered, and not allowed to infringe upon our rights. These are the real criminals, and they've escaped scot-free without any punishment for the crimes they have committed. Yes, our presidents have been evil, with mutilative greed, a want for power and control over hundreds of millions of people and to control them in a feudal state environment. These elitists are our country's real enemies. They want to destroy the Constitution to make themselves the masters of the world. It is a shame that many do not see this as they are so wrapped up in their self-indulgences and care not for their neighbor or their community.

If you want to know more about what I just spoke about, there is a book that I am currently reading that I would like to share with you. Each of these nonfiction books is heavy into detail about the East India Company from the beginning until now.

The Conspirator's Hierarchy – The Committee of 300
by Dr. John Coleman
also
Conspirator's Hierarchy: The Story of the Committee of 300
by Dr. John Coleman

I have been researching lately about the other communities of the world and it seems that many of the powerful countries are leaning towards the same lack of responsibility to their families and to their community. Within many different countries such as in Africa and China there is a strong sense of neighborhood and love of community in the remote villages and communities. When I was young, I lived in a Polish neighborhood and being Polish, I found a sense of love of community and neighbor respect. As I live today in a small neighborhood I am treated fairly, but my community does not permit me to join with them and to have any type of dialogue, and how I do miss this interaction.

Then again, I am also a slave of the United States government, which makes me feel I am no longer part of my community in this nation and under these circumstances I should be set free to move to another country such as Canada where others will receive me as they would be happy with me joining their union. This life of solitude eats away at one's soul, causing depression and other mental aberrations. And this was caused by our Department of Injustice. They took nothing and made the crime of which I am not guilty, and devastated my mental state and my physical being. One cannot know all that I suffer, nor do I want them to know, but need for them to be aware of what can happen to them if someone is to point a finger at them for a possible crime, because the FBI becomes vicious and worse than a frothing, contagious, diseased mad dog. They will keep hounding you relentlessly until one day they will have enough information no matter how small it is to put you away. I saw so many people at the resort who suffered this fate.

If my book saves one person's life from this kind of hell, I would find it a success, for I am into this book not for the money but for my way of restitution. I have also been encouraged, not only by my family and friends to write this book, but by others who know that these wrongs continue. These people have an intimate knowledge of what is going on and are looking forward to its printing. It has been said that this is probably the first biographical book that brings to light some of the misguided ways of the judicial system that might hopefully get some correction and so be it.

I live in fear and always in a state of constant vigilance.
It is what it is

My Health Situation

• • •

WHILE INCARCERATED I ACCRUED MANY medical problems. I did not receive treatment of the illnesses that I had prior to entering the resort. I was stripped of my pain medication for which I suffered immensely for the next three years and at times I could barely walk because of the pain.

I was given medications that I was allergic to which were sulfa drugs, causing serious interactions. I was also given insulin, but I did not know at that time I was allergic to this medication.

I contracted cellulitis, but they did not treat me as they should have and said it was not all that bad; then why would they put bandages on my legs and as soon as I got up from being re-bandaged with new cloth, my feet and socks were all wet and he said there was nothing wrong. This is the type of incompetency that runs supreme within the BOP.

In October 2014, I came up with an ataxic walk. Ataxic means clumsy and if you watch me I walk like a drunken sailor. This progressed into tremors and I was diagnosed in physical therapy that I had a high propensity for falling and was assigned a walker.

I used this walker for a period of time and then was told I had to go into a wheelchair and was pushed around the compound by a fellow inmate. They make a whole $25 a month to cart my ass around to wherever I needed to go.

In December 2014, I started to get the tremors. And they progressed to where I will get these violent tremors from anywhere from 15 minutes to two hours. Many times my body would freeze up afterwards and I could not move.

One time I had a severe case of the tremors and I had to stand up for count, which is mandatory. You stand there until everyone is counted. I was standing when my body went rigid and I fell to the floor. The guards came to check on me one time and the medical department never showed up. I laid rigid for over two hours on the floor. This happened several times.

This gives you some idea how inept the medical department is and is such today.

My point is that I came home a basket case and the solution has yet to be found as to what my problems are. It's not that the medical profession here at home is not trying, but my illnesses have become very complex.

As I understand it today, most of my problems are neurological and also psychological. I suffer from PTSD and other mental conditions such as depression, anxiety and others.

To determine what is really the problem requires a team effort and finally I am going to the Mayo Clinic to the neurology department.

I have placed a list of my illnesses prior to my incarceration and those that I garnered while I was there in this book. This will give you an idea of how badly they treat the geriatric inmates.

I told the judge of all my problems and illnesses and he stated that the BOP certainly will take good care of me. I consider that a bold-face lie. I'm certain he knows of the inadequate medical attention given within the BOP and by my going to this place, my illnesses were greatly enhanced and to work today, it is difficult for me to do anything. I guess I have to thank the judge for this and also the wonderful medical practitioners within the BOP.

I also know I have two types of cancer. I just found I have kidney cancer and an operation will be forthcoming. I also have what they call smoldering myeloma, which is a cancer of the immune system. I do have the cancer but it is not to the stage where it is being treated, and any day it could raise its ugly head and strike at me as it is an extremely aggressive cancer. It is rare, deadly, and extremely painful. I have these battles also to look forward to. I'm not crying about it, I am just telling you what is.

Each day is a struggle, but life is sweet and my wife who takes care of me, makes life wonderful. But the mental anguish that I suffer is deplorable. I have nightmares, day mares, battle with tremors and lack of balance, sometimes can barely walk, and worst of all realize each day that I am not free. I am property of the United States government and that to me is the most egregious sin I've ever seen anyone or any country commit. I have read about the slave trade, and today there are over 30 million slaves in servitude within the United States. Now you sleep on that one; I do every day, or try to.

It is what it is

My Health History

• • •

I was 68 years old, when I was first contacted by the FBI that I was under investigation. I have a series of illnesses and was taking a lot of medications at that time. Now I was taking a lot of medications, and I am allergic to a large number of medications with sulfa leading the way and if taken, I will have very serious reactions.

Before Arrest
COPD
Restless legs syndrome
Multiple myeloma, a rare, painful and deadly cancer of the blood
High blood pressure
Asthma
Type II diabetes
Degenerative arthritis in spine

- pain treated with opiate medication

Guillain-Barre Syndrome
Severe spinal stenosis

* pain being treated with medication until surgery

Pure hypercholesterolemia - under treatment – cholesterol levels under control
Spondyloarthropathy
Heart murmur

During my Incarceration and After Release
NO PAIN MEDICATION – SEVERE PAIN FOR OVER 3 YEARS

(*) Type II diabetes – not treated – A1C test was 9.4 after release – 7.2 is considered a high reading and is now causing major problems

(*) Cellulitis – hospitalized for five days and then for 14 days I had to go to the hospital for antibiotic infusions upon release. Infection received in prison and not treated properly

* chronic cellulitis –causing major problems

(*) MRSA - Contracted in the BOP
(*) C. diff (Clostridium difficilecolitis). *C. difficile* infection can range from mild to life-threatening. I am very susceptible to getting this infection again and bacterial medications for illnesses can be problematic

(*) Conditions of my *C. diff* infection includes:

- Watery diarrhea, up to 15 times each day
- Severe abdominal pain
- Loss of appetite
- Weight loss
- Can cause Ulcerated Colitis
- Geriatric individuals must be very careful in their use of antibiotics in the future, as they could have severe consequences. I was susceptible to this condition, because I have chronic cellulitis from not being treated properly.

(*) Movement control:
Ataxic gate –

- walk like a drunken sailor
- high tendency for falling

Loss of balance and vertigo while standing and walking
(*) Tremors

- Orthostatic tremors
- Essential tremors
- Demetria tremors
    - I have been diagnosed with the above tremors
- incidences of tremors vary in intensity and length of time; my whole body shakes violently from 15 minutes to 4 1/2 hours and my body has frozen up except for my head for from 15 minutes to 2 hours

(*) Balance and vertigo problems
(*) Mental problems including:

- depressive disorder
- high anxiety
- benign essential hypertension
- PTSD

(*) Allergic to Insulin
(*) Cancer of the kidney diagnosis – under treatment
(*) Degenerative arthritis in spine - pain NOT treated with medication
(*) Spondyloarthropathy - a disease of the vertebra – pain NOT treated with medication and no surgery
(*) Pinched nerves S1 – right and left side
(*) Severe neuropathy
(*) Severe spinal stenosis

- NOT treated for severe pain and no surgery
- have to sleep in sitting position, pain severe lying down

(*) Polyarticular arthritis – no treatment for pain
(*) Pure hypercholesterolemia - no treatment - cholesterol levels NOT under control
(*) Heart murmur
(*) Previously flaccid left arm
(*) loss of strength
(*) High propensity for falling and had numerous falls

Suspected kidney cancer – under surveillance – growth currently stable
Polyarticular arthritis

- treatment for pain

My attorney, prosecutor and judge knew of my illnesses, but I believe they felt it had no bearing at all on the outcome of my sentence.

You can see the minimalistic approach towards healthcare. Historically suing them in this jurisdiction has been futile and a waste of time, money and effort. Therefore, I share with you my health condition before and after my incarceration.

You will learn more about the terrible medical problems associated with the federal prison system, called the BOP (Bureau of Prison).

It is what it should not be

Health Problems

• • •

I WALKED INTO MY "NEW home of confinement" for a couple of years, walking in by myself and unaided, but when I left I was in a wheelchair being pushed by an inmate.

This is how far I deteriorated while being incarcerated, simply for lack of some medical attention, and an unwholesome high-starch diet

Prior to my incarceration, I had health problems and was diagnosed at that time with multiple myeloma, which is a rare cancer, is very painful and is deadly. It is by the grace of God it has not yet progressed to a point where I am being treated, but at any time this cancer can become very aggressive and will require immediate treatment.

I had a multitude of other illnesses such as COPD, asthma, high blood pressure, diabetes, lung problems, sleep apnea, and medical problems for which I needed to be under many doctors' care. That care was taken away from me during my stay at the federal facilities. I received minimal care and unfortunately most of the time that I was there I received no care and contracted some other illnesses that will plague me and hurt me for the rest of my life, such as cellulitis, MRSA, no treatment for diabetes (I am allergic to insulin and all medications containing sulfa, and they would not provide me with Januvia for my diabetes), extremely swollen legs and feet, ataxic gait, problems with severe pain in my ears, loss of teeth, stenosis in my cervical spine, tremors and others. I was even punished and retaliated against for my insistence on getting medical care. I tried and kept trying to get help, but they just avoided me. (*)

Now as if this is not bad enough, the facility where I was staying was a medical facility. They claim to have the best medical facilities in the world available for inmates, but I hate to burst their bubble, it apparently is one of the worst places to be. I have heard from other inmates staying in different institutions that their healthcare was far superior to this top echelon health facility as claimed on their website.

I will be delving into the other side of my life within the justice system in book 2. This book is just dedicated to the judicial part of it. Book 2 is dedicated to the BOP. And they are no better and possibly even worse than the judicial end.

The appendix at the end of this book will have a complete listing of my illnesses prior to being sent to the BOP and what my status is today as a result of their incompetence. I came out of the BOP a broken man physically, with emotional and mental problems created by the PTSD, but my spirituality is thankfully fully intact. (*)

I also suffered a lot of pain while incarcerated and was not given proper medications and while at home now, even though I have been prescribed serious pain medication, I still have a lot of pain. The new rules and regulations regarding opiates leaves me with a lot of high pain at times, but the joy of being alive and away from all those bastards makes me want to live to be 130, and to keep writing.

It is what it is

My Physical Illnesses

• • •

I HAVE SEVERAL ILLNESSES THAT are noticeable and announced to the general public; when these attacks, or as I call them incidences, occur they are not a pretty sight, but be that as it may, are real.

I received these wonderful gifts from my incarceration, which includes the sentencing by the judge with prompting from the persecutor and my do-nothing attorney. Also, blame goes to the medical department, especially one doctor and assistant health administrator at the medical resort where I was incarcerated. Now I am trying to get these illnesses under control and finding this process very difficult. My next step is to go to Mayo Clinic for testing, evaluation, hopefully diagnosis and possibly treatment. I live in this physical shell of a body that causes me great pain.

Is it not enough that I get a sentence that is ridiculous and held at bay under their parole system until the day I die. There are also other additives that I must live with. I am currently 73. During the time I have left on earth, I shall write, write and write some more.

Ataxia:

Many times, when I walk I walk with an ataxic gait. Ataxia means clumsy, but to tell you in simple terms how it looks, I walk like a drunken sailor. I must tell you that I get a lot of strange looks, but each time I get one of these strange looks, I feel so good inside because people I know have empathy and sympathy for me, while the nonhumans of the Department of injustice probably just laugh. Let them laugh, and that is the laugh of the devil and their being is now coming out.

Tremors:

This condition is not seen by many, because I really don't allow it to be visible or seen. Incidences have been seen in the hospital, but nobody knows what to do about them. That is the reason for going to the Mayo Clinic.

My whole body shakes, sometimes violently, as I cannot control these actions, nor stop them. Many times, when I speak, I stutter so badly that my words are hardly understood. These incidents last for anywhere from 15 minutes to 2 hours, after which time I am exhausted.

I've been told that I have these tremors at night, and I am talking sometimes quite loudly with the words being gibberish. I have found myself having a tremor attack and during that time I was "talking in tongues". This is not a language, but it is a language of inflections, tonal qualities, passionately spoken at a very rapid rate. My wife is mystified by my speaking this non-language, as I am when I hear it, as I do not and cannot control it.

Balance:

most of the time I do not have very good balance and even bounce off the walls, but that is better than falling. I have fallen quite a few times even with all the extra care that I take to prevent this incident, but it does not always work. After surgery and illness I lost a lot of strength, approximately 50% of my strength, therefore I cannot get up by myself if I fall and I need some very strong assistance. My wife cannot do it is that is an impossibility. So it's 911 time and great men from the fire department come over and pick my fat ass off the ground. These firemen are real gentlemen. Whenever I fall they assist me to make it to a designated area that I wanted to go to and make sure that I arrived there safely. They're wonderful people.

Pain:

I suffer from pangs of severe pain in my lower back and I take some narcotic medicines for this problem. I now visit a very wonderful pain specialist once a month, but I walk these days with heavy pain, and she is held under certain constraints by the federal government. Nor do I want to be pain-free; pain is an indicator of a problem and for something to go unnoticed could cause great problems, so I have learned to live with pain.

While I was at the resort which was a medical facility, they took away my pain medication and for three years I suffered immensely from pain. God damn their souls. These were the cruelest bastards.

I wrote this to give you some insight as to just some of the difficulties that I have because of their wrongdoings. I will just keep writing as long as I live about what the inhumanity of people in power causes to those who know not what to do, but suffer in their everyday existence. This country does not need these kinds of elitist.

It is what it is

In Harm's Way

• • •

Anyone who has been stigmatized with my type of crime gets a special bonus. We are classified as dangerous to society. In truth, the highest percentage of those that commit this crime are serious dangers to society, but on the other hand, others will have images on your computers, are guilty, but they are in a totally different league than those that lay hands on children and also those who try to control children to commit possible acts. These are the real dangerous criminals and should be punished severely.

With the advent of the changing drug laws, emphasis is being taken away from this crime, so another must be found to keep up the population within the prisons and this is one of the crimes that has been targeted along with beating spouses and drunken-driving, which have become federal offenses. The punishment for these crimes are in my estimation horrendous, but it fills this purpose of keeping the federal prisons full and in need of expansion. Again, it is all about the MONEY.

I am currently 73 years old, and had one child who died when he was two-and-one-half the day of his operation for a birth defect.

We also have another child who is healthy. When he was growing up I got involved in teaching hockey to very young children, because there were not enough coaches, so I volunteered. But hockey season was over, soccer started, and again not enough coaches, so I volunteered and coached for many years and had many winning seasons. I always loved children and helped to try to motivate them and talk to them in a friendly way.

Just before my arrest, I was working 12 to 16 hours a day, seven days a week on my companies, one which had a very large website that I designed and built by myself. It had over 5,000 items. Also, I had two distributing companies featuring hundreds of products in each, and I was the only sales person as I went around to different manufacturing facilities within the area to garner sales.

At this time, I was in my 60's and in relatively good shape, but I was not in my 30s and it takes its toll on my health.

The judge stated that he would look into my past to determine my criminality, but I guess he forgot to do such, because that has a bearing on determining what a sentence might be. This is called Mens Rae, which is part of the law. But I guess he was busy doing other things because he never bothered to check my background. The parole department did such and gave a recommendation, but he completely overlooked their findings. In my position, I find this unconscionable. And I am paying a heavy price for his absentmindedness.

To keep societies safe the dangerous criminals are required to sign up on a registry which is placed on the Internet. This creates a stigma on an individual without any forethought as to what this person is really like but immediately condemns him.

I have had rocks thrown at my house, barely missing the windows, as this is my working area overlooking the street. We hear bangs at night on the back of our house thinking, "here they are again, the deviants are attacking." People want to do harm, for laughs and giggles. I on the other hand, have a duty and responsibility to protect my family and I do not have the tools at times to defend myself as they have been taken away from me. Some things are amiss and those in power have not thought this through, but seems like simply a back room tactic without a bill to shuttle it through. I have to protect my family and I'm always highly vigilant, which causes me great and undue stress. I pray to God each night that they will leave my family alone, I care not much about myself, but their claim is that they love me and they stay with me and care for me as I need their help.

There was an incident in the grocery store where a man using his cart rammed into my knee while I was on the little motorized vehicle the supermarkets provide and then he ran off. A lady came over and was astonished at what she saw. She asked if my wife and I wanted to report this to store management, and she talked to them and they came and wrote a report.

All told, it's not so much for myself, but if any bastard messes with my wife, there's no telling what I will do. I certainly cannot be complicent to any crime, because I am not really guilty of any crime - if there is a crime it was perpetuated by the insane laws that are being passed on a daily basis. Yes, insane laws. Many are there for some very small minority of people whose social mores are more Puritanical than that of the Puritans. The bottom line is that my wife's peril is mine as well.

The other stupid part of this law or whatever you might call it is that if I was to go visit some relatives some distance away and I must stay there for a couple of days, after three days I have to sign in to the sheriff's office declaring my need to register. Well, where my relatives are, it is not conducive for me to visit them with this kind of stigma. Not only do I get punished by being in jail for a lengthy time, but I am further punished for the rest of my life for something I did not commit.

I have to deal with the circumstances and they just make me absolutely sick. It causes depression and other malaise, but do they care? HELL NO. They just take their liquid lunches and try to find a quiet space to take a little nap, and receive their bodacious salary. They really know how to fuck a person up to spend his time in hell on earth.

Perhaps I better close this chapter, because it is making me quite angry, and I do not need that.

It is what it is, but it should not be

Surveillance and Wire Tapping

• • •

WHEN YOU READ THE TOPIC of this chapter, I believe many of you are laughing. There's nothing wrong with that, because if I make you laugh, that makes me feel good. I love to make people laugh and I love to laugh myself. Unfortunately, this is all true. I digress…

My wife's sister was here visiting us over a weekend; she was in a back bedroom and came out and got my wife and said she heard voices in the room and men were talking to each other. One was saying to the other that they needed to get my wife to say something. We looked everywhere for these voices to find where they may have come from. If you understand my sister and my wife, they do not tell stories out of school. In fact, this made them very paranoid and wondering why the government would do something such as tapping into our private lives. I'm sure that there was no warrant, why should there be. The court will take care of everything; not to worry about things as small as a warrant.

My wife and I both feel that the FBI has tapped the phones, watching our computer traffic and have placed us under surveillance. Why? They apparently believe that I am the head of or part of an organization that deals in child porn. I'm sure that they recognize my skills as an organizer and would put these talents to work to make additional money. So, they do what they do: survey, listen and watch. Well, they have wasted their time and probably done many illegal things during this time. But who worries about the illegalities these days. Besides, what did they hear? I can answer that simply. NOTHING! I had a business to run and that consumed all of my time. So, I will just let them waste their time.

We believe that they have been looking and watching us even prior to my indictment. They were probably looking for me to be someone who, when caught, would rat or squeal on others within some massive organization. Boy, did I show them how wrong they really were. I was and am no head of any organization or even a member of any organization that dealt with child porn. (*) I was not in contact with anyone by telephone, by email, or by any related forums with others who were members of this type of group. It was a useless exercise for them to do this; however, it goes to show again my innocence. (*)

Or their surveillance could be a result of our former CPA having reportedly been in Special Ops and had been using my business for his own purposes.

What is the mantra of the Department of injustice? The basic element of everything is to find potential criminals, incarcerate them, and if an innocent person should happen to be one of those incarcerated, OH WELL (*) and will they do anything to correct the error, NO WAY. They are too proud and powerful to admit an error. (*)

THIS IS ONE OF THE MAIN REASONS FOR THIS BOOK.

It is what it is

Stealing Your Social Security

• • •

THIS ACTION ON THE PART of the government really **PISSED** me off. It is not enough that they have taken your life, but have now taken financial support for your family. This egregious act still bothers me immensely. The subject actually belongs in the second book, but you must know about it today.

The first day that you enter the BOP your Social Security is gone until you are released back into society after serving your penance. (*) Now your family has lost the resource to help your family and your children, as now they must fend for themselves. They have **STOLEN** your Social Security from you, as **I HAVE PAID FOR IT**. This is not an entitlement, this is money they're stealing from you that you paid into this fund. This just shows the greed and avarice of the Department of injustice as everything is based, as I have told you in the past, upon the **MONEY**. To me, **THIS IS THEFT**, and they are not even ashamed of this, as I say unto them, **SHAME ON YOU**.

Now most of these families could use this money for survival and now they must go out and get food stamps and any other entitlements so that they can survive. I do not blame them for doing what they have to do, but I do blame the BOP and the Department of Justice for their cruelty, there arrogance, their greed, their avarice and many other adjectives that I could expound on for the next 10 years. (*)

Let me say one last thing about the **STOLEN** Social Security monies. I was pissed when I found out that it was taken from me and I had no recourse. And today, I am still angry about this cruelty. **Who keeps the money?** I do not know, but let me take an educated guess that it probably is the BOP.

Again, I say, the Department of injustice has stolen my Social Security.

According to Wikipedia, in 2013, there were 2,220,300 inmates in the federal prison system. If one assumes that 5% was being collected from Social Security at a nominal monthly rate of $900 per month, someone would be receiving $99 million per month or $1.18 billion per year. I know a place where he could send a check to. Really, believe me, I wouldn't mind going to the bank and cashing the check and spending part of the money. I definitely would become philanthropic.

WHERE IS THE ACCOUNTABILITY AND TRANSPARENCY?

Remember, it is always about the **MONEY**. These people are truly **COLD**. (*)

It is what it is

Retaliation

• • •

WITHIN THE JUSTICE DEPARTMENT AND the BOP when a person tries to protect himself or obtain medical attention, in my experience it is not liked by the powers to be; retaliation can be and usually is enforced.

It is my supposition that when I had to go to court regarding my plea agreement, I wanted to protect myself from not spending a lot of time uselessly in a jail cell as I had a business to run and I did not perceive myself going to jail. So, I had the persecutor and my attorney sign an agreement that I would not go to jail after this event.

At the end of the session, the magistrate found out that I was not going to be imprisoned and became livid and was arguing with both the persecutor and my attorney as to why they made such a deal and stated that it was not within their jurisdiction that such allowances are made. However, since the agreement was signed by parties involved, the magistrate had to agree to it; however, he was going to pursue this matter further with the judge.

Later I heard from my attorney that their asses were severely chewed out for making such an agreement. It is also my belief that the judge may have received some unfavorable comments from the appeals court regarding this action. Judges do not like to have their asses chewed out, because it is beneath their dignity. Therefore, it is my supposition that the court had a prejudicial effect upon my sentencing, and everything they could do was done to increase my sentence and I believe stacking was involved as a form of retaliation.

The BOP is no different. My counselor upon my initiation into the facility told me that he hated me. During my stay there he retaliated against me several times, and one time, my attorney threatened him with some legal recourse and he stopped for a while. However, prior to my release, he made a big play by which he was going to get me in real trouble and it backfired. After the failed incident, he talked to me and told me that he was brought before the board along with other guards involved and they were punished for their misdeeds. I do believe he got some time off for his actions, and other participating guards also were reprimanded. Those who were also involved looked upon me with disdain. This was one active retaliation that failed.

My counselor also retaliated in many other ways and I will discuss those in book 2. I received assistance from influential inmates on my behalf, to his disdain.

I also believe that we received retaliation because of my wife's working to try and get my medical assistance which caused some consternation for certain key people within that medical area. Our house was robbed. Yes, our house was robbed while she was visiting me. This robbery is discussed in another chapter within this book. I realize that it belongs with the second book, but it was so egregious that I had to include it here to show how far some people go for retaliation.

It is what it is

Home Burglarized

• • •

My wife was working with an upper-management person within the regional office of the BOP regarding my lack of getting medical assistance. He is a very fine gentleman and saw to it that I received some much-needed medical treatment. Some people were humiliated by his actions as they were chastised for their lack of appropriate attention.

Medical attention was lacking in certain areas:

- not receiving proper medication for my diabetes, as I am allergic to insulin and all sulfa medications, making the choices few in conjunction within their restrictive limited formulary.
- Treatment with sulfa medications, to which I was very allergic, caused me severe allergic reactions.
- No treatment for cellulitis. They knew I had it but would not treat the disease. And today, I have chronic cellulitis and have to take high doses of a very expensive diuretic (the only sulfa-free diuretic on the market) and wear compression stockings day and night.

- No treatment for high blood pressure.
- No treatment for pain, as I had been treated for pain with a medically prescribed fentanyl patch prior to admission. Upon admission to the BOP I was stripped of the patch, and had to suffer the delirium tremors without any medical assistance. The prison system treats those addicted to drugs upon arrival, but I had to suffer alone and unaided, and it was very painful.

A visit was paid to the facility where I was housed by the regional office regarding my medical care. Because of this event, I received retaliation from my counselor, whose job it was to assist me and to help me with my stay at that facility and he did the contrary and was very abusive. This was not the only time that he took retaliation against me as I will discuss in the next book. (*) Also in the next book, I will discuss some of the doctors and their competence, especially one medical director of the facility who was terrible at his duties. He played the role of a doctor, but his training was reportedly as a surgical nurse. He was the cause of a lot of consternation within that institution.

My wife came down to visit me one weekend, and when she got back home the house had been robbed. After going through some of the details with her, I now feel very certain that it was a professional job and was done out of retaliation. The robbers seemed to be looking for a specific item as well as taking all of our valuable jewelry and ransacking all the bedrooms and the rooms we used as offices.

The reason I believe it was a professional hit is for several reasons. The scope of the search was very defined. The bulk of items taken were money and jewelry Some of the jewelry had great sentimental value and these damn thieves stole them from us. But the biggest reason that I am convinced that it was a professional hit was that they rifled through my desk looking for things and in my office drawer were two brand-new packages of Fentanyl patches plus the narcotics medication hydrocodone. A normal robber would gladly steal these items for his own use, or for sale on the black market. (*)

I strongly believe that they were looking for something, possibly a sim card from her cell phone because it contained some incriminating information – a record of calls made from the regional officer from one individual who was helping us. Research showed us that the prefix of the phone number was a government number used only on very special occasions.

I could easily give you three names of individuals who I think possibly could have either initiated or participated somehow in this illegal activity, but who, knowing the U.S. Government is involved, would assist? Nobody. Experience has shown us that even with proven illegal actions by our accountant, there was no action taken by local, state or federal agencies, as my wife tried all three. And also, there was no assistance given regarding my feeling that this was a professional burglary and retaliation. (*)

It is not a comforting feeling that agencies within our government would be involved in such illegal activities. I still believe strongly today that my comments above are all true. One would think I would waiver over the years, but my belief has become even more firm.

I am sure that nothing will ever be done about this invasion. The perpetrators will remain free while people like me and many like you who were law-abiding citizens are condemned for breaking a law that was not broken.

It is what it is

Friends and Foes

• • •

ONE WOULD ASSUME, AS I did, that after you served your time in prison, your friends would treat you the same as they did before. How wrong was I. When I got home, I tried to call several, including one brother who has shunned me and locked me out so that I cannot even call him. The rules and regulations of my release have changed my entire life, formerly one of happiness, productivity, and being a friendly sort of person. I used to love to make people laugh, as I would laugh with them. Sometimes the brunt of my laughter was on myself and I laughed even harder. There is no laughter today, nor has there been for a long time. Yes, I do laugh but with a very limited network of friends - my wife of course, some relatives and some very close friends who have not shunned me. But my social world is nonexistent today.

One other difficulty is that I will not allow myself to drive while in this condition and I rely upon my wife to take me where I need to go and this is causing an additional burden upon her for which I am very remorseful. I have been with her for over 50 years, and I love her dearly and also a few friends that remain. (*)

The judge made things virtually impossible for me to even have any kind of social life, or life outside of my home which

I call my prison without bars. I am still under the guise of the Department of injustice with the rules and regulations for the rest of my life because he gave me lifetime parole. With the same judge others who have committed a far more heinous crime than I had significantly less punishment than I have had, plus I blame the BOP for my conditions today with which I so painfully suffer.

I want to share with you two cases in which some good friends became unfriendly. (*)

One person, I call him now a person because he is no longer a friend and never will be again. I was a special consultant to the president of a very large company and did his bidding. No task was too large or too small. Within one of the divisions was an engineer who was somewhat talented, but his behavior was rather erratic. I was sent to the division he was in for at least two or three weeks at a time to calm him down and get him on the right track again or he would be fired. The president of this company did not really want to fire him, but this engineer was doing things out of line and especially displaying erratic behavior. It got so bad that the president called me to his office and stated that he was going to fire him. I asked for another time with him to see if he could be productive. He relinquished, and I got him back again to do what he was supposed to do in a manner that was acceptable. This went on five different times, and he finally quit and took a job at another place. I tried to help somebody and he shit on me. That is not the only one.

The point is that, I saved his ass many times from being fired and when I wanted to talk to him about my problem, he was nasty. I called him an ungrateful son of a bitch and left, never to see him again. I let somebody else put up with his erratic, irresponsible and violent behavior. Yes, violent he was. Really no great loss to me.

The person I am most disappointed with is the one who came to my sentencing and was ill-treated by the judge who was bombastic, demeaning and humiliating, and who was probably now suffering from the aftereffects of his very long lunch showing up 45 minutes late. (*)

I made this man millions of dollars. I was working at this one company as a consultant with the owners, or three brothers of Greek descent. Working with them was very difficult as we would decide upon something to make progress in a short period of time, and they would revert back to their old ways. My ex-friend was a very good consultant also, but he was Greek and this place needed someone of the same ethnic background, because these were not second- generation Greeks, but first-generation. I suggested my ex-friend quit his lucrative position with a large company and work with this group of gentlemen to turn the company around. He did so and after some short period of time (6 to 8 months), the company was sold for a lot of money and I know he received several million dollars for his efforts. (*)

I wanted to become involved and join him in several different ventures, but it never worked out and many times I was left in the lurch paying off debts. I was not treated very well as he promised some things and then went in a different direction, cutting me out. I felt this was not only fiscally reprehensible, but branded him as ungrateful and feel he is a "taker". He takes and takes and if you're really lucky you might get a little piece of something back.

I do not really want to talk about him, because he has a great family. But I tried to call him several times, contacted him by mail and email but I received no response. I am being shunned by him. (*) As I learned while incarcerated there are leeches or those who are called users, and now I classify him as one because he has used me to his benefit.

And in my research about this judge he spent very little time in private practice and I do not think he ever was involved in a trial. He grew up with a silver spoon as his family was very well-connected in the politics of the attorneys, and within a short period of time he was made a judge in the lower court and kept ascending in the ranks of POWER. (*)

With the edicts passed by this judge, I cannot even see my wife's cousins as we have been invited to many gatherings and I cannot go. As I cannot go, she does not attend these functions either. She takes care of me. And over two years after being released, I still need a great deal of assistance and care. I think God every day for her.

The majority of my friends have forgotten me, but I have a few that I dearly love. I do not want to mention names. There are two families that live relatively close to me that pray for me, as I so need it. Two of my three brothers I talk to, but they live a long distance from me and I cannot make the travel, nor abide by the conditions that are set upon me once I get to my destination. I will explain these later. My third brother is just like the rest of those who abandoned me.

An old fraternity brother and college roommate has contacted me many times encouraging me not to give up the fight. He was a major factor in my survival. There is also this beautiful young lady my wife and I met while in Italy. We sort of adopted her as part of our family, and she prayed for me and encouraged both me and my wife. There is one last person at home and I will be eternally grateful to her. I will always be eternally grateful to my wife, but also to her sister, who has helped out in so many ways. I can never repay her. Even today, when I have to travel for medical reasons, she will travel five hours to come to our house to help, as I need to travel with a wheelchair. My wife cannot handle this alone as I have lost a great deal of strength in my entire body and especially in my arms. I do not want to be a burden on them, but these two generous souls are my life's saviors.

We also have some very good neighbors who have also been good to us, and I again am eternally grateful.

You have no idea of the cloistered life that I live. The judge has ruined my life and cast upon me a death sentence and at the same time he has hurt other people, such as my wife, and that makes me angry. I do not seek revenge, as I am not a violent man. I do not worry about "getting even", as I am not a judge. God is the judge and all will have their day in His court. And may the fires of hell always be with him and them.

It is what it is

I Have Been Abused and Screwed by my Government

• • •

I HAVE BEEN SCREWED, ABUSED and many more adjectives by our federal government. I'm only talking about one segment of government, that being, the Department of Injustice, a.k.a. the DOI. This encompasses the federal court system, the FBI, the marshals and also the Bureau of Prisons, whose facilities I shall call "the Resort."

I spent over three years at "the resort" due to the ineptitude of the DOI. They are not the only one as there is one other individual who may have precipitated this ugly invasion of my life, which is now forever ruined, and embezzled from my company and probably will go unpunished.

I spent over a year and ½ doing research to back up my statements, but that is not quite necessary as we are seeing corruption, self-seeking edification, and profiteering by our elected officials and others who live beyond the scope of the law. But for the normal citizen, they want to feed the prisons.

Our country is not the only one in this predicament. If you look over in the EU, you will find that they have gone downhill faster than we have and if we do not make corrections now, the current status quo will get the ultimate goal of the one world order. A small group of people want to control your every movement, which includes your income, number of children you may have, what you can eat and how long you should live, but this is their mantra. This is nothing new, as it was started back in the 1700s by an elitist group of people, and can be traced back even further into the 12th and 13th century.

If you like to know more about the subject, I suggest you read any book written by Dr. John Coleman, especially those dealing with the Committee 300. If you would perchance read one of his books, read it with your eyes and mind open. What he writes about will shock you and that I guarantee.

I say up front at this time that I expect repercussions to happen to me regarding this book. But I need to get the message out as I am not the only one who suffers from this abuse, or worse. I also write this book for them, and for those that are to follow.

My misadventure of having been convicted of a federal crime has caused me, and hundreds of thousands of others, their lives, literally & figuratively.

In some cases, it is a real death sentence by which you will die and need to be buried; the other death sentence is for your banishment from society. That unto itself may be considered a death sentence, and you are looked upon as a deviant of society. Just because one has paid their time does not mean he can pick up where he left off, in fact, he had to start all over again with the monkey on his back.

In today's society they have programs, institutions, hospitals and other mechanisms for those who have a habit such as drugs or alcohol, but there is nothing to assist a person who has been taken

out of society for 10 years or more, because everything is changed and he has no idea what the current rules are. Because of this a lot of them end up back in prison, because now that is all they know.
It is what it is

Prejudicial Court

• • •

I BELIEVE ONE OF THE reasons why I got such a rousing, lengthy sentence is because of an incident that happened in front of a magistrate one afternoon. I was to be before the magistrate and via telephone calls with my attorney he told me that this was to be a meeting to set up the plea bargain.

I was asked the question if I was going to go to jail after I completed the session, and I said no. I did not trust them, so I told him that I wanted a document with his and the persecutor's signatures; they agreed, and I received it duly signed.

The athletic magistrate asked all kinds of questions that were self-seeking towards the government as they were pushing outrageously hard. Then the magistrate called time, for me to go to jail and stay there until my trial or sentence.

The prosecutor stood up and said that I could not go to jail because of an agreement that was made for me not to go to jail. The magistrate became livid, and that is being a kind word. I will say almost tyrannical, nasty and almost despotic.

In an argument, should I be polite and say it was a very vocal discussion; the magistrate was quoting rules of laws of different Circuit Courts, etc. etc. etc.

The end result was that I was free. But later I heard from my unambitious attorney that he and the persecutor got their asses chewed out quite heavily by the judge.

Now my supposition, as I do not know in fact, that I believe that the judge had his ass chewed out by the Circuit Court, which is why I feel such a robust and extremely harsh prejudicial sentence was given and imposed.

I believe that this incident caused them some difficulties and may have banded them together to make my life fucking miserable, and one way to do this is to extend my sentence far beyond where it should have been if I was guilty, but being innocent, the whole sordid affair is nothing more than BULLSHIT.

These are not nice people. I would never let anyone into my home, especially those from the Department of injustice.

It is what it is

Mind Control within The Court

• • •

THE GOVERNMENT DOES AN EXCELLENT job with mind control within the court. When you first walk into the courtroom, you will notice the very high ceilings, the dark paneling surrounding the entire court with muted lighting. In front stands this large desk or dais, by which the judge will preside. This design is meant for intimidation, showing power, strength and majesty. It is the blatant scene to humble you.

I was assembled within the court, and all is quiet and prior to the judge coming out from his room, quiet is ordered in the court as another show of force and power meant to intimidate you and tells you again who was the boss. After all are assembled and into their proper chairs, the bailiff comes out and in a loud voice announces the title and the name of the judge and for everybody to stand for the appearance of the judge. Once that is completed, the judge, in all of his majesty, enters with his flowing freshly pressed black robe. Finally, he will come from his room at his own pace and climb the stairs of his raised platform and take his seat on the bench and announce for everybody else to sit down. And now let the games begin. (*)

This whole scene is nothing more than acclimating the defendant to the power, omnipotence and regal majesty of the court and judge. In other words, it is meant to scare the shit out of you. And for the person being there for the first time, it is very effective. And each subsequent time thereafter, it has the same mind-numbing effect. All of the surroundings, the mannerisms and the show is orchestrated, just for the benefit of the defendant.

Only those who are experienced in the phenomena and have been to court many times obey its regulations, but does not demean the fear, the power and majesty as portrayed by these images and theatrics.

Then there are the procedures and policies by which the court functions. If you notice very carefully, the defendant is being controlled in a very obtrusive way.

It took me quite a while to figure this out and how this all worked. And it's all a part of the mind control that is used within the court systems.

I'm not saying it is good or bad or indifferent. I'm just saying that I believe this exists. I've been there. I've seen what was being done, and for a first-time defendant, I have to admit that it scared the shit out of me. It is very effective. But after a couple of times, the drama wears off and a more even playing field exists.

But as I said earlier in my discussions, mind control is everywhere, and everyone uses it whether they know it or not, because it is part of our mental structure to influence others without their knowing that we are trying to influence them. This is not always consciously done and most of the time is done subconsciously, but the fact remains, it is real.

It is what it is

Recidivism

• • •

Recidivism is a habitual or recurring relapse, and in this case a tendency to fall back into crime or antisocial behavior patterns. The program or plan to have incarcerated individuals become fruitful members of society and not to return to the penal institution has been difficult.

The Bureau of Prisons, BOP and the "Department of Injustice" always talk about what a great job they are doing in teaching and training their released inmates to become fruitful members of society, the goal being that they are not to return as a result of a crime. But they lie. Their failure rate is anywhere from 75% to 80% of inmates who return to the system as a result of crime. This means that 4 out of 5 will go back to prison.

Is it unintentional or planned? It makes no difference; they just don't want to spend the effort, the time and the monies to find these people jobs. Why? It is all about the money. It is easier to bring back an inmate who has served a multitude of years while incarcerated and put them back under the spell of their mind control so that they are mostly obedient and subservient inmates who generally follow the rules and regulations as prescribed by the prison officials. They want to keep the cash flowing into the pockets of the wealthy and powerful within the organization.

They really suck in this area, and it makes my blood boil. They are masters at inducing a hypnotic mind control over the inmates while incarcerated to keep them in a euphoric state without drugs.

When I went to "the resort" the only program they had was the GED program, but that is not enough. Their mantra at that time was that no inmate was to be released without at least a high school education or having earned their GED. This includes everyone and anyone and if they cannot speak the language, they must find an interpreter amongst the other inmates to assist them. As my time progressed, some programs were added with the assistance of talented inmates. They installed a computer system to teach inmates things like typing, Word and Excel. But the computers were not functional 80% of the time and to repair then was a lengthy process.

I did meet a couple of gentlemen that were not in my institution who reportedly had some decent programs tailored toward the inmates so that they could get a good job after being released. One inmate talked about having earned his license to work on Microsoft's products. This license is worth gold for that individual. And it can be for others if they only had the opportunity. He set himself up to go to North Dakota, where jobs were plentiful and his talents in high demand. He had success written all over him, while many others, or should I say almost all inmates, are destined for being at the hands of the unscrupulous BOP and will return shortly after they are released.

Another inmate that I met learned to be a cook. They had a culinary arts class at his institution, and while he was learning he would cook in the dining hall, or for the officials of that institution. I was getting hungry talking to him. This program is offered by very few penal institutions.

I purchased a book about the Bureau of Prisons, the rules and regulations regarding visitation and telephone calls and also what courses that they offer. Very few institutions offer any adequate courses that would be applicable for success in society. I was trying to find an institution that could help some inmates and better their chances of staying out, rather than coming back.

I got to know one gentlemen of elderly age, and he told me that he has no skills for work on the outside. I said to him that there is hope for you if you were to look. He had great communication skills and was great working with other people and could find such a job as a greeter at a place such as Walmart.

WHAT ABOUT THE INMATE:

The inmate does not stand a chance after spending many years in the prison culture, as one learns new ways of conduct which generally do not follow that of the culture and mores of the people that he will be associating with on the outside.

The inmate is not educated to assume the cultural roles for working within another and entirely different type of environment that he left and has forgotten much and how to behave, or garner the skills necessary for proper employment. There is a lot of talk within the institutions about these previously discussed items, but for the officials of the institution it is all talk-talk and there is no walk-walk.

INMATES ARE DESTINED TO FAILURE

No employer wants to hire them, no organization wants to have them within their fold and they are held under a short leash knowing that any time they could go back to prison for any innocuous reason. Generally, their social habits and that of society will conflict. Their social interaction with that of society is similar to going into a foreign country without the proper language. They have been surrounded by nothing but the prison language with its cussing and the overuse of one particular phrase or word that dominates any conversation, that being MF, as this serves as a noun, verb, or adjective comprising 90% of any sentence. I hated this word before going into the federal system, and hate it even more today, but this is one thing that will never change and for those released inmates who go back into society it will become a serious detriment.

Even the most hardened criminal, if they are truly remorseful, can adjust to be a stellar person in society, and his intentions may be good but the pressures he faces in society and their knowing that he has been taught a different code of behavior over the many years produces a conflict, and his adjustment will be very difficult and many times he will resort to his old ways and be back in prison. So sad!

I want to remind you that most of these gentlemen, and I use that term very loosely, are very bad people and for most, returning them to society will only invite another crime to be committed.

Can this trend be changed? Of course it can, but the "Department of Injustice" has no desire to spend the money, nor does it have the inclination and they are just too plain lazy to even attempt such a task. Many of these individuals who are in many different segments or parts of this organization are just as bad as the criminals themselves. Shocking? You know this is true; just open up your eyes and you shall see.

It is what it is

Norway's New System for Releasing Inmates into Society

• • •

Much of this was taken directly from the movie itself. This movie can be viewed on Netflix and I highly recommend it: Global Compass – "Prison: Breaking the Cycle" filmed in conjunction with The Economist FILMS @2015

For the inmate, the transition from incarceration to the social world is extremely difficult because while you're in prison you are used to making five decisions per day but on the outside, you are suddenly thrown into a position where you make five decisions every minute. This will cause a lot of consternation, confusion and possibly even irritability. It's going to take time for a former inmate to learn how to cope with this new environment and to relearn what he has forgotten.

A startling fact is that more than 50% of the prisoners released will eventually go back to prison again. It is not that they really want to, but is a matter of needing the tools to simulate themselves back into society and overcoming the stigmas placed upon them and following the guidelines from

the Justice Department that they must maintain in order to keep their freedom. If I did not have the support from my wife, her sister, my brothers, my fraternity brother and especially a few of my friends, including our special friend in Italy, I could've been a very likely candidate to find myself back in prison again. It is not that I want to go back, it is just very difficult to accomplish without assistance and their guidance. And whether you know it or not, you are still under the mind control of the BOP and it will take some time and great effort to rid yourself of that plague.

I find that in Norway they have a new technique that fits into a test mode by which they are teaching the inmates how to become good neighbors in a special environment.

Teaching **former inmates** to be good neighbors has many very positive results in that you are changing their habits that they learned while incarcerated which are antisocial and not neighborly. And there these Norwegian inmates have to live the life of a neighbor for a period of time before being released. Life in prison is not a social media but one plagued with dangers that can attack you in many ways such as: mentally, spiritually and physically; the problem is that you do not even know that this is happening to you; and the inmate himself not even knowing, this is an obvious clue that his mind is being controlled. (*)

In Norway, **"Punishment is the restriction of liberty: no other rights have been removed" "The offender has the same rights as others who live in Norway"** and life inside **resembles** this special facility, to live life as being on the outside as much as possible. This policy is being implemented in Norway, and allows the offender to at least have a chance of keeping away from prison while in the United States going back to prison is highly encouraged, (*) but it is very hush-hush. Nobody wants to talk about it but this is true in reality, as former inmates are not considered members of society. They are castaways, social trash and even considered evil people. I talk more on this subject in the chapter called recidivism.

The United States of America population is only 5% of the world's population while the **reoffending rate** is 77%, and is the highest in the world today. (*) (These figures are disgusting, but real). The United States now is competing with the past years of the Russian gulags, as we have far surpassed their range of terror, and no one seems to care within our own country. **Everyone has their eyes open, but they cannot see or most likely they do not want to see.** It is time that we looked at the problem straight in the eye and acknowledge our weaknesses and rebuild. A total restructuring is required. Piecemeal actions are certain to fail.

Comments:

Some of our presidents have taken a very hardline approach on the escalating laws being generated by Congress, and the driving force, which is money, is to increase our incarcerated population. The expanding number of laws have become exponential where even the most menial offense is treated with harsh punishment. Some of the crimes on the books today may be considered amoral or immoral to someone's social mores but there's no reason for punishment for them as the lawmakers are listening to their constituents and bowing to their personal agendas so as to garner their vote. (*) It appears that they're not looking at improvements, but rather giving out hard, harsh and in many cases unjust punishment just to fill the prisons and to keep the status quo and to satisfy a very small minority interest. And also, another very basic reason to increase the inmate population is for MONEY. (*)

President HW Bush purportedly stated: "They can go to jail, stay in jail and rot in jail."

President Clinton stated: "Three strikes and you are out".

President HW Bush's comment is having me rethink my position on him, and it is not positive. In fact, starting in the 1980's the incarceration rate exploded and has been growing at a rapid rate. Suffering from decades of hardline policy, the United States has 5% of the global population but it has 25% of the prison global population. Even Russia with its gulags **could not and cannot attain** such high heights of incarceration as that of the United States and so easily gain the top position of human beings incarcerated. For those of you who think this is grand, **PONDER** that you go to be incarcerated in one of these institutions and be innocent. I think this would be a good lesson, but I'm **merely** trying to tell you that I am innocent and I had to go through this horrible experience.

A huge amount of money is taken out of the hands of the taxpayer to build large complexes. The real reason why this condition is being supported, maintained, and reinforced is MONEY — the root of all evil. When you think of prisoners, think of money, lots of money, your money being wasted. The Texan judge Bobbie Francis has convicted his fair share of criminals and is not soft on crime. He stated that all you're doing is sending people to prison and by doing that you're sending them back over and over again. All you're doing is doubling the cost and crime rates go up.

Judge Francis of Texas has a program that deals with serial offenders who already have been convicted, and the recidivism rate in Texas has been significantly reduced. Now there are 250 of these programs all over the state of Texas.

Since that time, the state incarceration rate has dropped during that period of time.

The challenge for any country is to keep its offenders out of prison for good.

Until rehabilitation is put at the heart of any justice system's approach to punishment, they will continue to fail offenders, fail victims and fail society.

It is what it is

Global Compass – "Prison: Breaking the Cycle" filmed in conjunction with The Economist FILMS @2015

My Discussion - Life After Release

• • •

Here I stand before you, and one gets that many will tell you things that they don't want you to hear. But what I say to you is the TRUTH. But if they look at themselves deeply and honestly, they would have to agree with me, but certainly that will not happen. During my writings to you, I will say things several times over, but they are important.

After spending three years in a penal medical institution, as I am a geriatric with many health issues generated at "the resort" medical facility, I want to discuss some unintended consequences, or possibly intended consequences, of what does happen with the release of this inmate and the effects upon family and society.

I do not think that anybody has thought this clearly through because a lot of bad things happen when a person is incarcerated, for the really bad dudes and then also especially for those who are innocent.

I really don't want to talk about the repeat offenders because they have been stigmatized and have little chance of salvation.

The prison system changes everything about them; psychologically, physiologically, spiritually, morally and they have no idea of the changes that have occurred within society during their internment.

There mindset has been completely changed, as they have been relegated to making maybe five or six decisions per day and are then thrown into a foreign society that demands hundreds of decisions per day and some of these involve 10 or 15 decisions within five minutes. This simple fact overwhelms them, plus the euphoria of being free, but not really free, and keeps them shackles of the government. Their status within society has changed drastically and much more is expected out of them than they can possibly give. They do not have the tools, training or education to be productive as demanded by their former captors.

The only tool they have to survive is their instincts that they have honed while in the penal institution: that is to take what they need and to do unto others as they see fit. They have no remorse, no godliness and nothing to offer relating to working within society. They are entering an alien society, which they know little about, because time has passed by. This is why there is crime perpetrated by those released who are without any assistance from training for their reintroduction into society.

The BOP claims that they have a reentry program. You must remember that I was there for 3+ years and there is a significant amount of change that has happened on the outside that I was not aware of but had to get reeducated, not with the assistance and guidance of the BOP, but with my family and friends teaching me.

I will tell you what the BOP does for reentry. They have a three-day seminar and tell you before you possibly can go for assistance to get a job and what you HAVE to do so that you will not return. I would like to grade the programs for reentry. My grade is F minus. My brief for medical, especially for geriatrics is again F minus.

What is the greatest overall? As I keep telling over and over again, it is all about that MONEY. Deep down, the administrators care less about them being successful, but would rather have them fail. Why? Again I keep telling over and over it's about the MONEY.

When President Trump said that the Justice Department is broken, no truer words were ever spoken. What to do about it is again a very simple answer, to entirely revamp the entire system, because now you know where the unintended consequences lie and can correct with better programs, which are now a dismal failure.

They must be vigilant with the violent offender's reentry into society. They must have at least a chance to earn a decent living yet be reportable and their actions checked for compliance. Does this sound simple, while it is because I'm sure it had been discussed many times, but goes against the grain of current conventional thinking, which unto itself has gone askew.

"This country used to have a proud history of law enforcement." This statement is BULLSHIT, and is really stated by those who have something to hide. The justice system in this country has always been skewed and has been notoriously subversive to the Blacks, and the laws governing the people, especially involving those who have committed crimes, and was emulated by countries all over the world, and yet today it is equal to that of a 1/4 world country and our incarceration rate has gone through the roof.

And the most important thing is what have we done for those that were committed to a penal institution, for doing a crime or for those poor schmucks like me, who served time and have to spend the rest of my life on parole. If you do not take a plea bargain as devised by the court and go to trial, you are penalized with the doubling of your sentence. One has no choice but to kowtow to their demands. How do I know this? Remember, I was there. I experienced it, as my attorney told me that he would not take me to trial because he would lose and that the prosecutor is far better in court than he is. My faith in the justice system fell apart. And now I suffer a life of illness because of lack of proper medical care within these institutions. To put it bluntly, I live in another prison, but one without bars. I am watched very carefully, much more than a mother watches her child, while others who are far more dangerous are left alone.

Not for me to be selfish is not what this is about. It is about those who have served time in a penal institution and the ramifications it has upon them. Firstly, for the older citizens who are under some type of Social Security, the money paid into it by you is taken away from you when you enter the institution and you no longer receive the benefits that could easily help with the family's financial burdens. You can get a job working in UNICOR, (a prison labor program for inmates which is a wholly owned United States government corporation), which makes products for the institution but also for the Armed Forces and recently products are being sold to the general public, such as eyewear and furniture. These consumer goods are competing in the marketplace today, but with cheap labor. This topic will be discussed in detail in my second book.

The family now has to survive on its own and has lost a major part of its financial resources and many of the other important family needs such as the love and discipline by a male figure head.

The family structure is destroyed because the disciplinarian is no longer within the unit and it is recognized that the children often grow up in the footsteps of the father, and then they will in the course of time either join gangs or unto themselves, commit a crime and then be placed in jail, and the beat goes on from generation to generation. I have seen father and son in the same prison; that was a very sad day.

The other missing factor is that of taking a potentially productive citizen of the community and making him and the family a burden on society. This man can no longer contribute or earn money and therefore by definition is a burden. He now is incarcerated and is costing taxpayers money; therefore, he is a burden and is not a disciplinarian to keep his children from following a detrimental path. Society shuns him when he gets out and when he tries to get a job, and in most cases that can't happen; that's why he reverts back to what he does best, crime. The important point is that he is in an educational system where he learns his new trade and is released. His education comes from Penitentiary University or PU, or BOPU.

Let's take another look at our judicial system and my perturbing case. There was no discovery, no mens rea, a useless attorney and most importantly their mantra to maintain their 98.6% incarceration average. We need to look back into our history where we respected each other, talked, and were friendly. I have watched old movies and I love watching them. I grew up in the 40s and 50s without television. We did not have all the amenities of today; we can bring it all back together again if everyone just showed one thing that I really learned in prison— it was RESPECT.

It is what it is

Cost of Incarceration

• • •

I BELIEVE THERE IS AN important factor that you need to know as I've always talked about money and it is an important element. My topic now is about your money, not the money that I was speaking about within the book. A lot of that is ill-gotten money. This is the money that the taxpayers, such as you, have paid for my incarceration. I do not thank you, because I did want to go there in the first place.

So, let's look at the first important item. There are four classifications of health within the BOP system. Each class is based upon the inmate's current health status.

Code 1 - is perfectly healthy inmate.
Code 2 – inmate with some health issues but nothing that requires any major resources.
Code 3 - are the inmates with serious difficulties such as, cancer, heart problems, lung problems and many other illnesses that require regular hospitalization or hospital treatment. These are serious illnesses. There are two places where these inmates reside. One is within the hospital proper when an inmate needs attention all the time and others in other institutions who need to visit the

hospital on a periodic regular basis. This is an area where I stayed and visited the hospital on very rare occasions.

Code 4 - this is the hospice inmate and they have a special section within the hospital for these individuals. There are also other institutions around the country that service basically as hospice homes for the dying.

Let's talk about money.

Code 1 and Code 2- is allocated a budget of about $30,000 per person for the year. That includes your meals, clothing, beds and other normal expenses.

Code 3 and Code 4 - with an allocated budget of around $100,000 year.

What I'm trying to make apparent here is that I was a Code 3 and was generating over a hundred thousand dollars' in income through a budgetary process for my stay there.

    I don't know what you think about this but I have my own idea. I don't think I need to share it with you because you probably know what it is and I don't think I would be too far wrong to make the assumption that we were are not only in the same church, but the same pew and singing from the same songbook.

I just thought you'd like to know.

Parole

• • •

WHEN YOU ARE ACCUSED OF a crime and released from prison, you will and must report to the probation office under their terms. Prior to sentencing, the usual terms are that you must meet with your parole officer at least once a month and sometimes more. However, if you are accused of anything that has to do with alcohol or drugs, you must report to the parole office for drug and alcohol screening, by which you pee into a little cup. If you are "dirty", or have alcohol or drugs within your system, be sure you tell them that you are dirty before you pee in the cup. It may go a little bit for you, but if you do not tell them you are in big trouble. You are at the mercy of the parole office. They can either admonish you, and you better come back clean the next time, or you can become incarcerated. That is their decision to make; there is no recourse. You have violated the tenets of your parole. Also, the parole office at this time, if this is your first offense, will dig into your financial personal history and make recommendations to the court as to what they feel your sentence ought to be.

The recommendations that the parole office gave to the judge in my case was for three years on home confinement and he gave me four years within an institution where I did not get the medical treatment I would have if I was under home confinement.

After you have served your time and are at home, there is some time that you must spend on parole as dictated by the omnipotent judge. When there is failure to comply to the tenets of the parole office and their dictates, the judge can send you back to the penal institution, usually for a year and one day. And when you come out, you're back on parole again under the same rules and regulations in effect until you have completed your parole.

You are now in society and an unfree man. You have a lot of your rights taken away from you. There are many things that you cannot do in your invisible handcuffs and shackles that bind you to the Department of injustice for the rest of your life. As if that is not enough, you are legally a slave to the government of the United States. That's right, you are a slave, pure and simple, under the 13th amendment of the Constitution of the United States. I will discuss this in future chapters, as I feel it is a very important subject, especially if you love freedom as much as I do. It burns at my soul, at my very being, my everything.

Sorry, I digress… We are finally out and away from captivation and the steel bars. You are now under the guise of the probation office and to obey their dictates. In most cases if you work with them they work with you. They are not the ugly monsters that put you in this position of incarceration in the first place unless you have disturbed such. I'm only talking to those who have been incarcerated because of whatever the reason may be.

I must admit that my parole office and parole officer have been good to me. But again, I do not go out deliberately breaking the tenets that I am bound to by the overaggressive judge with the rest of my life on parole. If I was deserving of such a cruel penalty or punishment of being on probation for the rest of my life, I would have no problem accepting my fate, but the sentence is so far out of kilter with the norm that I struggle at times to find rationality behind such an ignominious decision by this person and I wonder why?

    I have to admit that the parole office that I am assigned is fair and my parole officer I do respect. You all have a difficult job, especially those who do not want to follow the rules, and their rules are the only rules that count. Your rules are nonexistent, so get over it.

        It is what it is

Three Felonies a Day

• • •

You may not realize or even want to admit that you commit at least three felonies per day, but you do. Sorry to burst your bubble, but facts are facts.

I know that you are not aware of these felonies that you commit. By law you are supposed to know about them and not commit them. You are supposed to be attuned to all the laws that pertain to you as we are a country of laws. Since the 1980s, with President Clinton and the three strikes and you are out program, the number of laws have exploded. To make matters even worse, there is no repository or database contained for these laws so that you can educate yourself. At last count, I believe there were 6,600 laws on the books. How you are going to adjust your life so that you are compliant with 6,600 laws is beyond the scope of my comprehension.

Just because I made these remarks, I need to justify my position, and my position was reading the following book.

Three Felonies A Day: How the Feds Target the Innocent (Paperback – June 7, 2011)
by Harvey Silverglate (Author),
Alan M. Dershowitz (Foreword)

The average professional in this country wakes up in the morning, goes to work, comes home, eats dinner, and then goes to sleep, unaware that he or she has likely committed several federal crimes that day. Why? The answer lies in the very nature of modern federal criminal laws, which have exploded in number but have also become impossibly broad and vague. In Three Felonies a Day, Harvey A. Silverglate reveals how federal criminal laws have become dangerously disconnected from the English common law tradition and how prosecutors can pin arguable federal crimes on any one of us, for even the most seemingly innocuous behavior. The volume of federal crimes in recent decades has increased well beyond the statute books and into the morass of the Code of Federal Regulations, handing federal prosecutors an additional trove of vague and exceedingly complex and technical prohibitions to stick on their hapless targets. The dangers spelled out in Three Felonies a Day do not apply solely to "white collar criminals," state and local politicians, and professionals. No social class or profession is safe from this troubling form of social control by the executive branch, and nothing less than the integrity of our constitutional democracy hangs in the balance.

This book is available on Amazon.com.
It is what it is

Born a Free Man but now a Slave

• • •

OF ALL THE THINGS THAT I have been through since my release from that God-awful place called the federal prison, this is probably the worst thing that has happened to me. I am now classified as a slave, and I can appreciate how the blacks have suffered with this stigma.

While incarcerated, I did not know of the amendment that makes all felons slaves upon release. It is the 13th Amendment to the Constitution of the United States of America. I am constantly watchful and fearful of what others are going to do to me, my wife, my family and friends. Some bad things have happened to me after release:

- Weirdos walking by my house because they know where I live, because I have to tell the public that I am here according to some of these overly zealous laws that have been produced.
- Having to suffer people running into me with their grocery carts, then running away like a slithering rat.

- The inability to visit with relatives, because some of the laws imposed do not allow for me to do such.
- To live a lonely life, although I have my wife of 50 years and a few friends, but just a few of the many that I once had, many of whom now shun me. It is not so much the shunning that bothers me, but it is a fact that they, my old friends, resort to such condescending attitudes as they are better than anyone else. I thought I had better friends than what I have, but to find out most of them are "takers". They wanted me to give to them without reciprocating. I find this and them rather disgusting.
- With the very poor medical treatment that I received, I have been battling for the past two years to regain part of my health. My wife is also my caregiver, my mentor and everything in my life now revolves around her as I need her. I do not drive very much because of the conditions that I have and I do not want to harm anyone, therefore I rarely drive.
- I have received retaliation within the injustice system and also within the BOP. But the most egregious was when our house was robbed, and I feel it was by some people in the government or associated with the government who are responsible. Will nothing be done about it? Are you kidding? They protect themselves, don't you know that? If they robbed there will be no retribution from me, because the government will do nothing about investigating. I leave it up to God to be the judge as He sees fit.
- There are many more items that I could discuss; I try to live my day seeking peace.

- In my time on earth, of 73 years, I hope to see a book displayed within our country. I have seen despots in documentaries with their cruelty to the people which I find very appalling. But, in this country, this was never to be expected. But, my wife and I have been recipients of some of the cruelty more than one could ever imagine. I can imagine cruelty coming from a person or small group of people, but our government with the finest Constitution that ever has been devised by man has just been trashed. What a shame! (*)

I digress… All the above, each unto itself, is egregious; combined it is grossly egregious with peril. But, for me to find out that I am no longer a free man but a slave stunned me so badly that I went into denial of that fact. For some reason while I was incarcerated I became interested in the slave trade. This is natural because I was surrounded by a lot of black men, and some turned out to be amongst my best friends. I was a sickly guy and they took care of me. They gave me clothes if I needed them. They showed me their way of life and it was most fascinating and I learned so much from them, and I told them things about themselves that they did not know. These were things that are not in any history books, but you have to be a person who likes real facts in history, and that's me, and also being very curious about anything and everything.

After having read three books about slavery and finding out that I am now a slave not only turned my stomach, but my brain went almost dysfunctional. It was a tragic shock. The reason being is if you are born free, you know what freedom is. Now let me take that freedom that you have away from you and give it to me. How would you like that? Would you fight for it back? Would you just forget about it? What would you do?

There are people who fight for their freedom and sometimes when they get their freedom they don't know what a gift they have or what to do with it because it is so intangible and so real that it absorbs your very being and consumes you in the euphoria. (*) The euphoria so big that it could crush you. One could lose reality that they could not control this new freedom. It is so awesome that to be taken from you with the stroke of a pen and knowing that the person next to you is not like you. They are free, you are not. Now do you understand why I feel so fucking sad, remorseful, angry and many other adjectives that cannot adequately explain how I feel? (*)

I understand why and what was done, but that law should have been changed many years ago. I am sickened to be a slave, I want my freedom back. I know I'll get it back when I die, but I want it now, today, not tomorrow. (*)

It is what it is

Good Morning Slave

• • •

It is a horrifying, debilitating and unbearable feeling within your stomach that I spent 69 years of my life and the only crimes committed are a few speeding tickets and possibly a couple of parking tickets which were all paid and now I am charged and convicted of a heinous crime to spend years in a federal penitentiary. Upon my release and doing some research regarding my current position, I find that as a graduate of a federal penal system I am now classified as a slave of the United States government according to the 13th amendment of the Constitution.

There are no special conditions for this new role in society and thought that I had served my unjust sentence and now find that I am no longer free man.

Now some will say that that is an old law, but it is a constitutional law regardless of its validity or not and is still a law. Senators, attorneys and politicians always speak about this country as one of laws. I realize as you do, that many of the elitist within the country do not pay attention to the laws as they feel they are above the law and are not responsible for their actions.

I have the ball in the case where I am not an elitist, therefore, if there is a law I have to observe it or be condemned for committing it's supposed crime. As all laws, many are unjust, unqualifying and quite frankly, just plain stupid. But as it stands at this moment, I AM A SLAVE dictated by the laws of the Constitution.

This amendment was crafted in order to give everyone, White, Black. Red, Yellow, freedom under the eyes of the law and to abolish slavery. That was the intent and purpose of the 13th Amendment, but some changes were made and never corrected, nor will they ever be corrected as they cannot afford to at this point in time. And I will tell you why an egregious error was made with the signing of the 13th Amendment.

This was a period in history when cheap labor, vis-à-vis slave labor, was considered to be a necessity, so that the plantation owners could have their stately mansions and their white-gloved parties as the work was done on their plantations with minimal expense of labor, being slave labor. This amendment to the Constitution emancipated the Blacks from slavery. But anyone who has been confined within a federal prison or penitentiary for any reason and has served their time and is released then becomes a slave to the federal government, and they can place them anywhere to do the bidding of their new masters. These new slaves may not be Black, but can be White, Yellow, Brown, Green - any color under the rainbow, but in fact it was designed for the black members of society released from prison to serve as cheap labor for these plantation owners. Unfortunately, I am appalled from once being a freeman, sent to prison on a charge of which I did not commit, and now I am marked as a slave to the government that I love. I am sickened by this.

You might say that is passé and this practice is no longer utilized. But the law still exists, and we are a nation of laws and one would think that this is quite laughable, but not I, for I take this charge very seriously and I feel as if now I am a slave.

Slaves are still being used but with great secrecy. The person or persons drawn into this web will never be heard from again. There are no rights for the ex-felon, and by a simple knock at the door one can be taken away forever under the condition that he has no rights as a slave.

Every morning when I get up, I say to myself, "good morning slave". Do I really believe this? Absolutely. And it has for the past two years tormented me every day of my life and as I go through each day, this has a bearing upon my psyche and causes me depression.

This amendment was created after the Civil War, and a special amendment was made to placate the plantation owners. It was begrudgingly signed by Abraham Lincoln. The plantation owners would not go along with this amendment unless they could find a way of getting their cheap slave labor and this was a compromise.

This law still is on the books and active and could be rejuvenated at any time. But what I cannot take is that I am at this time 73 years old and suddenly from a freeman I became a slave. It is very hard for me to accept; I loved my freedom. You grew up with freedom, understand freedom, live in freedom, love freedom and suddenly you are no longer free. This is extremely hard to bear, and I know that you do not understand, but is probably one of the worst feelings I've ever had in my entire life that I am forced to live with it until the day I die. Only death will set me free.

Now let's go just one step further. While I was incarcerated, I was abused, tormented and even retaliated against and when I got out, I was acting rather strange and not my normal self and come to find out that I am suffering from PTSD and other psychological issues. I've yet to be cured of this psychological malady, even after two years I still suffer. And one of the things I suffer about is this attitude of my being a slave of my government. It is the thought that becomes so depressing, making me even more depressed than I really am supposed to be, but I can't help it.

If you put yourself in this same scenario, how do you think you would act?

Something must be noted: I really don't think that many people know about this situation, it is only because I'm writing this book, and in my research I came across this horrible law. While I am suffering from this disease it has taken hold of me and will not let me free. It bothers me all the time and I do wake up and I say "good morning slave," and I need to let it go, but it is real and this is no fake mind game I am playing.

There is something about PTSD (post-traumatic stress disorder) which is very relevant. I have talked to several sociologists and psychologists, in particular talking about my mental problems in PTSD. They have told me that PTSD is quite common for released inmates who are older, that the elderly suffer from this mental disease, especially if they are innocent. There are many serving time today who are innocent.

ALL I WANT IS TO BE FREE, AND NOT BE A SLAVE
                       It is what it is

From a Freeman to a Slave

• • •

I WAS ONCE A FREE person just like you, enjoying the free life that is given to you and me and endorsed by the Constitution of the United States of America. Now with a stroke of a pen and an amendment to the Constitution, I have become a slave to my own country. This means that I am a slave in and as a slave to the government United States, as they are my master.

I want to share with you my experiences, my feelings and my turpitudes of what I believe to be cruel and unusual punishment dictated at the hands of several departments within the Department of injustice. What you read is reality to its fullest extent. I will not sugarcoat my message to you, as now I feel as a cast out of society similar to the person in "The Scarlet Letter" written by Nathaniel Hawthorn.

My feelings on the subject are deep and very hurtful. This transgresses to my very soul and I believe in fact that I am no longer a bona fide member of this country called United States of America, but rather now am that of a slave living in this great country of which I used to be a free citizen. My heart and my soul cried within my brain the rejection that I so poignantly feel and I must live this way for the rest of my life. One cannot imagine the sorrow, the anguish, the bitterness and how this poisons my very being.

While incarcerated I read several books about slaves and the slave trade that even today I take time to read to see what is happening currently, and it is truly ugly. I feel their despair, but, there are some differences. They were torn away from their people, their culture and their community, which is a huge tragedy. I now personally understand this tragedy when a person has lived within a free society within a great country and is suddenly made a slave by the stroke of a pen and from then on is forced to serve according to the wishes of the master.

I am currently 73 years old and have been out of the structured walls of a prison for over two years, but now I am being held by the invisible tentacles of this country's Constitution as a slave for the rest of my life. The only release from these chains will be when I die. Any person released from the federal justice system is or will be serving the same fate as I am today, is a graduate to becoming a slave. But now, because of this action, my health and psychological being has deteriorated. Depression is a common mental illness that has been imposed upon me by this new title.

I used to love to walk, but am now bound to a wheelchair or a walker, and for the most part I am relegated to a life of near-solitude. I'm taking this time in writing this book so that you might understand what happens to a person after returning from prison, especially to those whose crime is determined to be outside of the social mores of current thinking, as it has been hell and continues to be such and will be until the day I die. I have written this book for many reasons, and basically it is a testament to what is wrong with our society today. In the past it was not such, but it has gotten progressively worse, and within the last 50 years it has slowly escalated until it has reached its pinnacle today and growing at a rapid rate. The issue of slavery was done after the Civil War with the great Emancipation Proclamation as a sidebar to satisfying the southern plantation owners to have a steady supply of cheap labor.

The axiom that "you are innocent until proven guilty" is now, "You are guilty and must prove your innocence"; if you fail to prove your innocence, they will penalize you with additional jail time, which is illegal, but is practiced on a wholesale scale.

The chart shows the number of people incarcerated in the world and the United States has a very poor showing; it ranks as number two and only is superseded by Seychelles which has the highest rates. This is something not to be proud of.

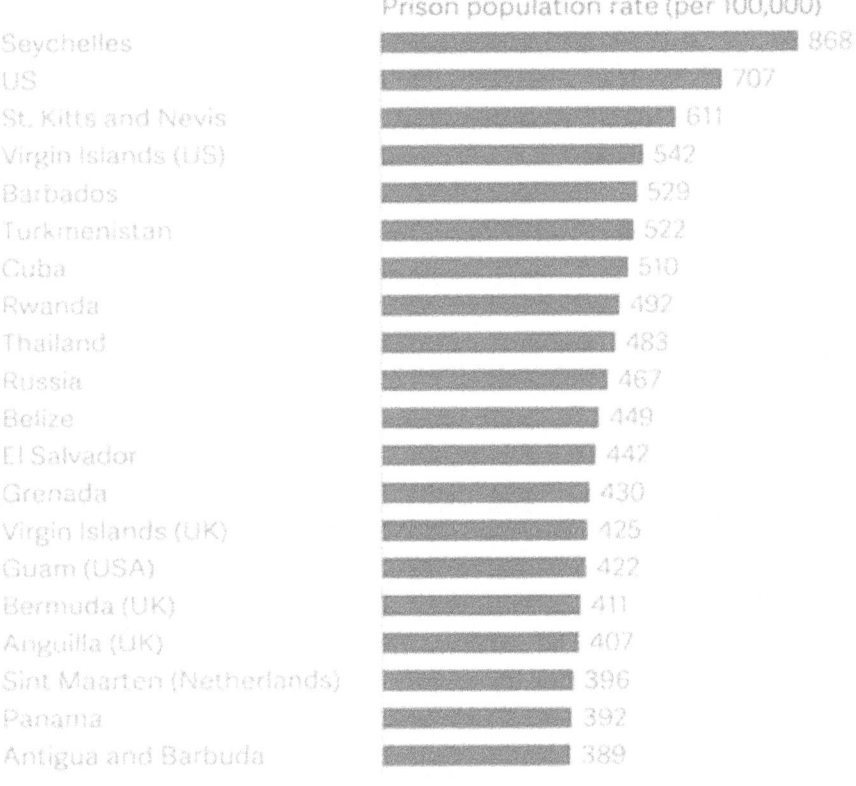

The most incarcerated countries in the world

Prison population rate (per 100,000)

Seychelles	868
US	707
St. Kitts and Nevis	611
Virgin Islands (US)	542
Barbados	529
Turkmenistan	522
Cuba	510
Rwanda	492
Thailand	483
Russia	467
Belize	449
El Salvador	442
Grenada	430
Virgin Islands (UK)	425
Guam (USA)	422
Bermuda (UK)	411
Anguilla (UK)	407
Sint Maarten (Netherlands)	396
Panama	392
Antigua and Barbuda	389

I have decided to document this tragedy. I hardly believe that progress will be made towards rectifying some of the wrongs that have been misguided. There are organizations, politicians, religious people and other interested parties that are trying to change the misguided efforts of a few for their own personal agenda. These powerful forces will continue to thwart any progress that has been done very recently, but things will change.

There will be more writings regardng all persons who have done their time but will forever be monikered as a slave of the United States government.

It is what it is

Slavery - I Want to Die a Freeman

• • •

I DO NOT WANT TO die a slave but a free man, and part of this chapter is relevant to that point, but I also will discuss slavery in general as to what I've learned about this most cruel condition placed upon a human being by another.

For some strange reason, I feel a close bond, probably because most of my friends were black, and I am white. But since I was a child, I was colorblind as skin color meant nothing to me but only the color of our hearts. And some of these black friends have become very close to me, and I to them. I shall never meet them again because I cannot, but if I could I certainly would. We taught each other a lot, as I told them things that they did not know about their current situations and how all of that arose. And they told me about their magnificent existing culture that they now share.

For 68 years, I lived as a free man under the Constitution of The United States. I was sent to federal prison for a crime I did not commit and was literally forced into taking a plea bargain. My attorney would not take me to trial because he said the prosecutor will pull tricks and convince the jury that I am guilty, even though I am innocent.

After my release, I went home to my wife of 50 years to find out that I lost all my friends except for a very few. Many will not talk to me anymore or even recognize that I exist. I call my current environment a prison without bars, in that I am held by the guidelines of the edicts as imposed by the judge and also by the edicts of the parole office as delegated by Congress or the Justice Department. Living life is not good mentally as I am in a prison without bars, but to make one error, and I would be back in a prison with bars for an inordinate amount of time.

I suffered and my wife suffered for their abuse, cruelty and retaliation. Yes, we were retaliated against. I was in captivity like a caged tiger, and she was and is working hard to try to help me and while I was incarcerated, our home was burglarized. I was not there, but I feel from her description and photos of our ransacked house that this was a professional robbery. I feel it was done to send a message and also to retrieve some incriminating evidence, which we still have. We also believe that we have been wiretapped and all our actions have been watched, but they couldn't find anything, and I still think we are being watched and wiretapped today, and they will find nothing. Why? Because we did nothing nor were involved with any groups associated with the claim I was supposed to have done. No proof, just speculation and forcing me to take a plea bargain, of which they are experts in completing.

I was doing research to do some writings before I was incarcerated and enjoyed looking into some conspiracy theories. I did not necessarily believe in them, but they were of interest and my interests are so varied and so diverse, but they are just interests as I am curious. I have been like this all my life and my curiosity never ceases.

Then I come across the 13th amendment, which stipulates that all men are free and this is the amendment that makes Blacks no longer slaves. The country is now neutral except that if you are released from federal prison, you are now a SLAVE of the United States government as your new master. This amendment to the Constitution was for the large southern plantation owners who needed cheap labor. So, when they got out of prison they were made to go back working on these farms and plantations for a very meager wage. The inmates also work for a very meager wage and there are persons behind these organizations that make a lot of money.

My point of this initial discussion was to give you some insight as to my feelings and show how I still feel I'm a slave, and I relate with feelings of the other slaves of this world who unjustifiably have been condemned to a world of servitude. Their master has complete control over their life or death and can and do kill those who are not productive. But, in the past a slave was worth a lot of money, so harming a slave was not profitable. Believe it or not today's lives are cheap. There are about 30 million slaves just in the United States under servitude to someone from anything from housework to prostitution. I have found empathy with these people and I despise those who have them.

How Slavery Started

In Africa, according to my readings, tribes would war with each other and the winner would take whoever was ever left in that village - the men, women and children - and take them to another place to sell them into slavery. This next tier usually was within Africa run by a big tribe on that continent and they in turn would sell these poor people to another organization which in turn would sell them to ship-owners who then took them out of their native country to their new final masters.

Slavery is no different today than it was of yesteryears. Slaves come from wars, or even kidnappings and are sold for profit. This practice goes on today.

I have read about a ship of slaves they transported from Africa with a drop point in the Virgin Islands. This today is even a transfer point. The life on ship is deplorable, food and water is scarce, there is a common toilet which is nothing more than corner of the belly of the ship and death is common where the bodies are disposed in a nonhuman manner. They are just thrown over the side of the boat as a meal for the sharks.

Excuse me for being so passionate on the subject; we will live in luxury to not see those that are hidden behind the curtain doing manual labor for their master, or prostituting themselves for a pimp's financial gain.

Being a slave, I continue to fear the government or its agents who could come to my home and take me away, for I have no rights, to a place I will never be heard from or seen again.

So, as I write this article or chapter I am sinking lower and lower into the higher states of my depression because I do not want to die a slave. I want to die a free man and I know this court has not one ounce of compassion or reality. But I also want all of the slaves in this world to become free, and their masters and the traffickers severely punished.

        It is what it is

Slave – Yes, but How to Succeed

• • •

So, you see, I believed that once you finished your sentence, you had paid your debt to society and are free to resume your previous life. My dear readers, you are so very wrong. You have only started the second part of your journey and this portion will go on for the rest of your life. There is no such thing as freedom after you are released and supposedly paid your dues to society.

The first day when you leave the federal institution with your discharge papers, you think you are free and that is BULLSHIT. You have just been initiated or signed up unbeknownst to you, to a growing group of individuals such as I for the rest of your life. There are no dues, but rules. Congratulations, you are now a slave of the United States government. (*) If you have it in your head that you are now free, let me be the first to tell you, you are so very wrong. You're wrong as now they have you exactly where they want you.

- You have lost your right to vote, but in some states that ruling is being overturned. And the government really does not want to see this as I will explain later in this chapter.
- You have lost your right to bear arms. They don't want to see you around guns. Why? Because you literally scare the shit out of them. They worry that some may get together for some foul deed. And being you do not have any rights to some protection, do you think they're going to come out here and help you if you have a problem? I need not answer that one.
- You may have lost some of your rights to free speech. One is just a lackey of the government again.
- You cannot be in contact or call or associate with any other felon in any manner, which includes letter writing, emails, telephone calls of any kind, meeting on the street corner or any kind of meeting anywhere. I have known of some people who have been sent back to serve more time because they were talkative to fellow felons. It does not make a difference what the discussion was, now you can't do that.
- You cannot communicate with anyone that is presently in a federal institution or graduate thereof, unless you want to go back and enjoin your friend in the institution for an extended period of time, and I doubt if you will be put together, but you will both be widely separated.
- It has been told to you that all efforts have been made and even laws have been made so that you have the opportunity to get a job when you are released. BULLSHIT! (*) They

tell you this to make you feel happy, and are free to tell the truth, because you're going to have a very difficult time finding and keeping a job. A non-speaking English refugee will have an easier time than you will have.

I offer you a solution, as I do not want to see you suffer or your family suffer, as you and your family have suffered enough, unless you are really a nasty guy, then I say unto you, fuck you.

I do admire a man who has changed, for the better. My suggestion is for you to find something that you can do and are good at doing. This is what I have done, GO TO WORK FOR YOURSELF. Many have made it and are doing quite well and so can you. Do not fear the unknown. Embrace the future with all you have at the beginning. To start a business takes a lot of hard work and effort, confidence in yourself and it will keep you out of trouble. Just make sure that the business that you're going into is legal. Hint: drugs is an illegal business. Stay away from the booze and drugs; they will catch you and you don't need them around. Concentrate on your new future and really concentrate on your family who may not have forsaken you. Start a donut shop across the street from the police station, is the first thing that comes to my mind. Keep your initial idea simple, and expand from there when you have the monies to do such.

I'm going to give you some big hints.

- Do some volunteer work.
- Get involved with your community
- Get involved with your church and go to church with your family

- Forget the partying, which serves no purpose and is not productive
- Hang out with community groups and not on street corners

Now for the biggest hint of all. When you have your business started, and have a direction and goals of what you want to achieve within your business, find someone that can help you write a business plan. It does not have to be fancy or in any special format and visit with the group associated with the Chamber of Commerce called SCORE.

Score is a group of individuals of retired businessmen. They have the skills and knowledge on how to run a business and make it successful and they volunteer their services to others. I am thinking about joining this group in the near future because of my extensive business background. I have saved companies from failure plus I have my own company that was destroyed when I was sent for internment.

You must remember one thing, that many are extremely paranoid and they fear for their safety. I guess I can't blame them in some ways. But there is a dirty little secret here that you don't know about - 25% of our current population in the United States has been incarcerated for one reason or another. (*) This is hundreds of thousands of men and women who have suffered the same fate of being in jail. That is a healthy voting bloc. And this is why they do not want past inmates joining together. And I can understand their point, but then again, I can't.

I heard this comment made or written about several times is that the unions would like to have all the felons join with the union. That would give them awesome power. But I doubt this would ever happen. But if it does happen, I would be tempted to join.

There are of course special conditions given to very special ex-inmates, such as I. I have to register myself once a year with the local sheriff letting everybody know that I am a target to be abused if they so desire. I've already had rocks thrown at myself, and rammed by a supermarket cart, with this deviant driver scurrying off like the disgusting animal he is. A rat has higher status. And I'm always on the watchful side, because it is my goal and responsibility to protect my wife from these evil morons. I have seen more intelligent animals within the monkey farm than I see sometimes on the streets.

You possibly think the powers to be, such as our beloved congressmen and senators have the power to think past their nose at some unintended consequences they create with their "laws" that are being pushed by some innocuous group in order to garner their votes.

I will get off my soapbox now to tell you there's probably more. The powers to be that supervise your release will enlighten you. I have found that the people I am involved with within the parole department have treated me well. The judicial department has screwed me. I just must tell you, but there are some good people out there and they are not that bad. Work with the good ones and shun the bad ones.

By the way, I said many times that I am 73 years old and in poor health, but that does not stop me from working. Currently I'm working 10 to 12 hours a day, seven days a week on this book. When this is finished, I will start my second book on the BOP and after that two more books. I do not have time to party since most of my friends have forsaken me, I don't need them in my life. I found out that I'm reaching out to many others by sharing what I know and have researched.

My last comment to you is one that I made earlier: concentrate on your new future and really concentrate on your family. May God bless you all.

Mind Control - Introduction

• • •

WHILE IN COLLEGE I HAD minors in philosophy, psychology, sociology and through my many years I've always had this habit of observing people to see how they affect what they do, as I was very curious. I have a very curious nature. There is nothing out of the realm of my curiosity until this day, because I do not get out that often as I am in a prison without bars. I will explain this in another chapter.

My theory about mind control and what's going on will probably cover several chapters because I don't want to make each one of them too long and lose your attention. I feel this is rather critical information as I find it is so real. I was quite shocked upon realization what I found. I did more investigation into some of the strangest areas one could ever believe, and some do exist in the real world.

While I was at "the resort", a.k.a. a penal institution within the BOP, I had plenty of time to observe people and this was one of my favorite hobbies. Over a period of three years, some things became very apparent to me because they were highly repetitive. I saw the same things over and over again and I looked at other realities, realizing they don't fit into the norm that exists on the outside.

I attribute using the name "resort" as the institution of my incarceration to my attorney who represented me in the state where I was imprisoned. It is the term that my attorney used in his correspondence and also I will use it as a form of respect to him. He is the kindest and one of the most benevolent persons I have ever known in my entire life.

My observations became more and more intuitive to try and find some common reasoning as to what is transpiring. Suddenly one day, like any other day, it seemed like a lightning bolt permeated my brain and I suddenly understood what was transpiring.

The reason for such tranquility and obedience became very apparent as to what causes this phenomenon. It's not just being locked up behind a bunch of wire; it's much more than this. Actions of the inmates are kept in control was my answer. Then I started questioning myself, was my supposition correct, or am I delusional. So, I took some time out for some rationalization and found out that I was not delusional but something here exists and now I know what it is. It is mind control; all inmates are under a form of mind control.

So, my research there went a little bit further and further and I was making notes. My full attention was to write a book about this phenomenon, and the title of the book was to be "Flesh Robots" because all of the inmates walked around as if they were toy soldiers. Which reminds me of Tchaikovsky's *March of The Toy Soldiers*, and I would go around singing the melody to this symphony.

The more I looked the more I learned and indeed they were all in their form of mind control and it was induced and planned and implemented by the BOP. It was a technique to keep the inmates under control without the use of force or harsh punishment

Actually, as I observed, it was quite peaceful without problems most of the time where I was housed, because they were holding at bay a lot of alpha-1 males of many different races, colors, ethnic backgrounds, different educational levels from the poorest who can't read to PhD's all contained within this unit.

To me there was a standard that was quite humorous. Some background first. I was in a low facility, where there was supposed to be a more-or-less relaxed atmosphere and the inmates are not in a real situation of flight. But around the compound was a wall called double-wire. There was one surrounding wire all the way around the compound, and 15 to 20 feet away was another wire all the way around the compound and each of these layers contained upon them huge serpentine wire that would cut your body to shreds if you tried to maneuver through them. The chances of escape are nil, none, nonexistent and all inmates knew the physical barrier surrounding our living area. The humorous anecdote was that the fences were built to keep the public out. We were not aware this has a merit to it, because all of our needs are taken care of. We had a bed, admittedly quite bad as the mattress is only about an inch thick on a steel plate. We were given clothing and responsible for it and it was to be maintained in a clean manner and of course, there were three meals a day. The meals were not home cooking, far from it, as we ate a lot of starchy foods such as rice, rice and, more rice. At times there were special meals which were, I have to admit that were not only delicious but wholesome.

And for this reason, there was a saying that the wire was to keep the public out. It was one of those things that made everybody feel better, because there was so little good news. This being a medical facility there was all the death, quite a bit, and mishandling of people quite a bit and depressing it was.

I digress...

Now that I've given you the background of why I believe strongly that we were held under mind control as a method of keeping peace and controlling the inmates, I want to explore with you in another chapter more about mind control in other areas, such as the judicial system, which is heavy into it as I've come to realize.

One last thought about this chapter - the mind control that was subjected to me both in the judicial department and within the BOP still wreaks havoc with me, and I find myself drawn back consciously or subconsciously into these dark days. I guess that is part of the problem I am having with my diagnosed PTSD and I must eliminate this evil within my mind.

It is what it is

Mind Control II - What is it?

• • •

Now that I have breached the subject of mind control, do not think of it as necessarily an evil, as it does have some positive merits to it. It becomes evil when it's used in evil ways as it has been.

Mind control basically says that one person or an organization is using some type of technique so that it controls another person or organization without their knowing it and has that other person or organization follow the direction of the originator of the control.

For example, take a wife in a family who wants her husband to do the dishes at night. Boy, am I going to get in trouble over this one. Over a period of time, because it does take quite a while for one to be effective, she starts sending out little signals, little nuances, of how delightful it is to do the dishes, and does not make it sound like drudgery, but delight. And the kids join in to make it a happy time, and pretty soon the old man is going to come over and ask if he can help. What has happened is he is helping with the dishes. Do you go further so that he does them all the time? This may not be a really good idea, but if he helps, you know you have communication. This is a time to talk and discuss things and make you closer to each other. What a wonderful thing.

Now did you use mind control to be abusive? No, you used mind control to cover something even better for the both of you. Use mind control for good and not evil; there's enough evil in this world as it is today

Mind control could be used for a good purpose. However, it seems like the only people that really use it are the destructive ones and why is this? It is because they do not want the general population to know about this technique. It is because it is greatly used by others. And if you look at yourselves deeply enough and seriously enough, you will find you are in some form of mind control whether you like it or not. You will not realize it because that is the way it was generated: for you not to know, but just to do. Just as the wife convinced her husband to assist in doing the dishes, he never knew what really hit him, or understood why he was doing this. But the facts remain she had caused him to assist in one of her chores. And there is nothing really wrong for him helping her with the dishes.

There are many times that you, without even knowing, are using mind control. You yourself don't even realize you are causing a circumstance for another person to do your bidding without their knowing it. And if you look deep enough into yourself you are going to find out that you have achieved this goal, good, bad or indifferent. You are not even aware of what you are doing. In many cases this is not a learned trait, but some people just have a knack for doing this, and they understand that they have this type of control

Mind control is a natural event within our minds. You are affected and you are affecting others, mostly at knowing what you did.

I have kept the first chapter positive, because there is a very sinister side to mind control, and in fact if you go deeper, it often becomes quite evil, but we will not touch that right now.

It is what it is

Inmates

• • •

I happened to remember that I spent 3+ years with a group of people who have been signified as the dredges of society. Most have committed terrible crimes, but some are innocent. Some are good people, but so many are bad while others are the worst of our society.

There is harsh realization that where you are placed in one of these institutions, your life is in peril, especially if you are older, sickly or committed crimes that do not meet the standards of others. Yes, certain crimes have different ranking according to the offense involved. Those that have dealt with drugs, are at the upper echelon of acceptability, while other crimes are considered heinous and many times these inmates are treated with extreme cruelty and some have been murdered as the result of their crime, yes, murdered.

The inmates have their own rules and are different in each institution and almost all are different by the risk value of that institution. The penitentiary, has the strictest codes while the camps being low risk institutions are considered safer, but you are never really safe, ever.

One must enter these institutions, in my estimation, without fear. I feared no one or anyone when I was introduced into the general population. The inmates smell fear and will take advantage of you no matter what your age and the geriatrics are the most vulnerable.

My three-year stay within the institution was deplorable. You <u>do *not*</u> understand <u>*or cannot*</u> understand what it is to live each day on a 48-month sentence. It does not sound like a long time, does it? But it is. You are without your friends and family, the comforts of home, the joys of working and there are also the social gatherings of your peers that are now only a memory.

When I was sent to these institutions, I went without fear, knowing that I might have to fight for my life. And there were instances where my life was in peril. But I must thank some of my friends, who protected me.

In prison, you are surrounded by a bunch of really bad dudes, along with those who are struggling to survive, but you do make some acquaintances, prison friends and lifelong friends. Stay away from the bad dudes. They are usually gang members and M13 is the worst gang, but I did learn something about it even in prison. They are subject to the guidelines and rules and regulations of that of the hierarchy and must get permission to commit certain crimes within the prison institution. They cannot act on their own.

Then you have the acquaintances and these are those you can talk to but only in general topics. Personal information with them is personal as they can and will use it against you. Then you have the prison friends who you can associate with but you must be very careful about talking about your past. Remember that you are in a group of people who will snitch on you for their own betterment without any remorse or apologies.

Now that you have your friends, there is a time when you have had some trust with them and they with you. If they do not share their past with you, do not share your past with anyone. Some of these inmates have been together for many years and become very close friends. I was fortunate to find several special men to whom I would consider my close friends while in prison. One man gave me a long-sleeved shirt, as I was cold. They gave me special meals to eat with them. They socialized with me and treated me as one of their own. And they served as my protectors. These gentlemen, and I do call them gentlemen, are all members of a very powerful gang and one was a leader. He and I formed a special bond that will remain with me the rest of my life. Strange how things happen.

When you are released from prison, one of the conditions that you must adhere to completely is never visit with your friends again. You cannot call them, write to them or contact them in any way, because if you are caught both will attend jail for a period of time. I know this to be true, as I have seen inmates who have returned because of this violation.

I also have found out, that being an ex-con, felon or whatever you want to call me, gives me a different status within the outside community. These days that stigma can be good in some way and bad in a lot of ways. Understand that this population is growing rapidly and now is a huge minority, with over 25% of the population of the United States being felons. They don't want you to vote, because they fear that this huge minority can change and will change the outcome of many elections, so they stifle the movement towards organization because of the sheer numbers and a common background of being a felon. This is why they do not want released felons to meet. To put it simply, they fear the potential consequences.

In my next book, I want to share with you some of my friends. I will not give you their names; it is not necessary. Their personalities have given me a wonderful experience into a world of social rejection, denial of a decent job, hassled by their past and bound by some very strange rules imposed upon them as a condition of release. People say they have paid for their crime, but that is a bunch of BULLSHIT. The punishment goes on until you die. Other societies make amends, but this country today continues to monitor, observe and use your past against you in many ways. They want your servitude and seemingly do not want your success.

I will always be held under the thumb of the federal bureaucracy of the United States as a slave in more ways than one. They do not want to see you or me succeed, only to fail, as that is their mantra. We are heading back towards the feudal system in this country. Take off your rose-colored glasses and observe and educate yourself. Beware of those selling snake oil remedies.

I would like to discuss the opposite side, or the evil side. Inmates have a lot of time on their hands and they contrive and think of ways to earn illicit money. I read about some of the methods by which they accomplish these nefarious gains. In my estimation, these inmates need to be placed in something that I would call a solitary situation, where they have no correspondence at all with the outside world, PERIOD. Because what happens is that now this activity is proven to be successful and now it becomes a classroom subject by which other inmates are educated to steal.

I have no use for these people, none. These are the real lowlifes, who will revisit the penal system time and time again after being released. Some individuals just need to be marked off, not killed, but unable to do any harm to themselves or to others. **These are the dangerous people.**

                              It is what it is

Disgrace

• • •

For the past year and one half I have been scouring the Internet for information for this book and I encountered a large amount of information which is staggering. I was so surprised to find so much information in many different ways and yet, no one notices, no one reads, no one really seems to give a damn about it. ABOUT WHAT?

The problem within the justice system in the BOP has been going on for many years. One of the major obstacles that perpetuates its ineffectiveness is that of the sentencing guidelines. Prior to these idiotic requirements, the judge made his sentence on what he felt best according to that of the person charged, the person's background, the social mores of the area and many other factors that entered into his decision. However, whomever has taken the judge's responsibility to judge and passes it along to the persecutor, who now controls the court. The judge is really not even required, as a secretary could pass out the preordained sentence as prescribed by the persecutor.

Justice, you call this justice, is the abomination of the Constitution of the United States. The founding fathers would be turning over in their graves to find a group of men sitting in a smoke-filled room joking around and making up sentencing for individuals they know nothing about or anything about their crime, and this passes on as the law of the land. This is no law of the land. This is no law at all, but now it is nothing more than a monkey court.

You call it the country of laws. This one factor of sentencing guidelines has made an abomination of a past highly respected judicial system. Shame on you. Shame on those who pass the stupid law and shame on those who participate, because they are not God. You certainly cannot call this the country of laws anymore, as it's been turned into a sham.

One thing has always bothered me about the sentencing guidelines and that is why are you so surreptitious in calling them sentencing guidelines, when in reality we should call it mandatory sentencing. Trying to scare the shit out of people to not committing crimes, don't sugarcoat it. Tell it like it is. You will go to jail for this amount of time. Now the judge doesn't need to be there because the secretary could hand out the sentence. And thinking of that, you don't even need the defense attorney. I would not need an attorney; I didn't have one, but did have one masquerading as one, but the whole show was run by the prosecutor. Let's be honest once in a while, or is that possible?

On the other side of this dissertation is the unprecedented growth of the number of laws being made by our Congress. It is strange for me to find out that the Congressmen or Representatives do not even look at the laws that are passed as they seem to be conceived and made in the back rooms by clerks, secretaries and maybe even the janitor; the new bills are attached to a bill that is shipped through Congress without those responsible not even knowing what laws are being passed that affect the lives of the citizens. Again, I say shame on you. You took an oath to do your best for those who elected you and you do nothing to protect them. Why is this? Too many power lunches?

Make the laws so that all citizens know what the laws are as they are responsible to remain in compliance. But it is a known fact even a first-year law student could not comprehend but only a small portion of all the laws that are currently on the books. Also, the number of these laws being passed is exponential. Soon it will be against the law to brush your teeth at certain hours, it's getting to be that ridiculous.

Please, tell me where a citizen can find a database with all the laws, the offenses, a short explanation so that an eighth-grade child could understand them that is viewable to the public. They do not know the answer, I do. There is nothing available. You are asking the citizens to know all the laws and yet you keep them secret. Shame on you.

Do you think my little discussion ends everything? You think such? Shame on you. This is only the start. But maybe, just maybe, complete one of the above and to me that would be a monumental achievement and the founders of our great country just might smile upon you.

We Live Our Lives In Real Fear

• • •

Since 2012, we have lived in a state of fear, and do so even today. When I was first accused of my supposed crime that I did not commit, I was initiated to fear and I live that life of hell even today.

Not knowing or understanding what my future was to be caused me great consternation. I try to remain strong, but some of the forces are just too strong by which they not only ruin your mental state, but also your physical being.

Through this ordeal, and at this point in time I suffer from many illnesses, both mental and physical, and I have been trying to get assistance for many years, but other things have interrupted the diagnosis and potential cure for these maladies as yet to be determined.

The abusive treatment that I received within the BOP exasperated my physical illnesses and undermined my mental health. They refused treatment for my diabetes because I was allergic to insulin and required a medication that they would not provide "due to cost". Their deliberate non-treatment of cellulitis caused a chronic disease which I will battle for the rest of my life. I also had MRSA in this BOP facility within a year before my release.

Within a month after release from this prison, I spent time in the hospital for recuperation from cellulitis followed by twice-daily infusion therapy for two weeks. They had to rid my body of infection before I could have an operation which was imperative or I would lose my ability to walk. Then, the operations itself caused me additional problems as I got weaker and lost much of my body strength. I was told the surgery should have been done much earlier to lessen the chance of this problem, but due to the fear of infection, my surgery had to be delayed. Again, this all started within the BOP. I not only attribute these illnesses to the BOP, but to the judicial system that sent me to the BOP. The parole board, realizing my tenuous nature at the time of my sentencing, recommended quite a different sentence of home confinement by which I could receive proper medical treatment, but I now suffer as I am today and probably will for the rest of my life.

I fear several things. Firstly, I fear that one day someone will come knocking at my door and take me away. The reason why I do not know at this time, but this is a major fear that is causing some of my mental problems. There is no escaping this fact, and I have announced my fear to those who would listen. I have seen so much cruelty and abuse not only within the Justice Department, but even more so within the BOP. It was a living nightmare, and I have these nightmares and day-mares every single day of my life and it causes me fits of depression and tremors which are at many times severe and I have been trying to seek treatment.

I not only fear those who have put us into this position, but also by the restraints that I have been placed under and, as there are causal effects that now threaten me and my wife's very being,

I fear those that wish to do me harm. I am not so much concerned about my welfare, but that of my wife. I have been punished for supposed sins that I did not commit, and she is being punished for loving me and taking care of me for the illnesses garnered through the justice system. WHY IS SHE BEING PUNISHED AND THREATENED? This is against the Constitution of the United States as she is entitled not to be put under such duress, nor should I. This is an egregious law and is unconstitutional and the makers of such laws should be punished for their unconscionable acts.

You have no idea of the mental anguish and physical pain that we go through every day of my life. Even today, we feel like we are being abused, because I have to live under conditions that placed me and my wife in harm's way, which is totally unconscionable and I believe unamerican. I do not believe that the Constitution of The United States made by our forefathers would allow such a circumstance. We are now ascending into witch hunting, where a person is condemned for a crime that is not a crime. Because looking at my sentence, it is based upon "intent." One cannot be condemned for "intent", as an action must happen for a crime to be certified. This law has condemned me to a life of fear, pain and misery for the rest of my life. How cruel, how ungodly cruel, when the Constitution stipulates that no one should receive cruel and unusual punishment, and I am a living person being persecuted.

My wife and I have no power to do anything but to sit here and to be accosted, mentally beaten and possibly physically, and without hope.

YOU HAVE NO IDEA OF THE PAIN, THE SUFFERING AND THE DESPAIR THEY HAVE CREATED.

WE LIVE IN FEAR!

THIS IS WRONG!

IF SOMETHING SHOULD HAPPEN TO MY WIFE, I DO NOT KNOW WHAT I WILL DO!

THIS IS VERY WRONG!

I Shall Never Bow to Tyranny Again

• • •

SYNOPSIS OF SICK ME AND STILL FIGHTING

PRIOR TO MY INDICTMENT AND incarceration, I had well managed medical care and was a relatively active person of 68 years old. I did have a cancer called multiple myeloma, but it was not to the stage where they would start treatment. And for some reason unbeknownst to many doctors, I am not yet in a position to be treated for this cancer. In this I am very fortunate and thankful as it is a very terrible and painful disease.

Prior to my entrance to a specific institution within the BOP I was walking. Previous to my incarceration and while still at home I tried to walk at least one half-hour per day for exercise. However, when I was released to home confinement for six months after finishing the sentence imposed upon me, I spent most of my time in a wheelchair. I regressed from walking to being in a wheelchair, and my health deteriorated after I came home. I spent many days in hospitals because of the illnesses that were acquired while in the BOP and because I was not given proper and timely medical care while a guest at "the resort." I now needed drastic medical attention and was battling for my life and required high-powered medications.

One of the major illnesses I acquired in "the resort" is cellulitis. Cellulitis is a bacterial infection that is also related to MRSA and C. diff (a very difficult and lengthy infection to resolve), which I battled for about a year.

When I had another flare-up of cellulitis shortly after coming home, it was intense. My legs became extremely swollen and red again (they had been fire-engine red for a good part of the time I was in "the resort" along with the swelling and at times the blistering.) This time I was fortunate to be home and was admitted to the hospital, put on IVs for six days and for two weeks after this was given infusion therapy twice a day. It took an hour in the morning and evening sessions for this medication to be infused into my body.

The medical facility at the BOP where I was an inmate failed to recognize that I had a problem with my neck, in which I had severe cervical stenosis. I was told I needed an operation as soon as possible and needed treatment quickly or I eventually would lose my ability to walk, but it wasn't until a year after my release that I could have this surgery because it took this long to rid my body of this infection which I had received in the Bureau of Prisons. If I did have the operation with cellulitis in my body, I was in big trouble, as the disease will attach to the hardware and open bones requiring subsequent operations. While incarcerated, I had this infection frequently, but it was only treated once and that was when I had MRSA. These infections of cellulitis, MRSA and C. diff are plagues that surround any hospital or medical facility. It requires diligent care with housekeeping and isolation of the patients to try and eliminate the source of an infected area.

My wife and I, along with my attorneys in the state where I was incarcerated, battled the BOP for my medical care. My sentencing judge assured me that I would get excellent care in the BOP; he lied to me. This is unconscionable. The illnesses I had prior to being sent away are progressing because of my lengthy stay within the confines of the BOP and they have exacerbated my medical conditions that I have today.

Because of my many different conditions and the effect they have on my body, I did not allow myself to drive when I was released because I did not want to hurt anybody, nor myself. The reason being that I could fall sound asleep at any time for short periods of time. I would be in conversations and talking to people when suddenly without warning I would fall sound asleep. Even after a year and one half of being free of the BOP, I drive only very infrequently. My poor wife has to cart my ass everywhere, and I do see a lot of doctors, along with physical therapy.

Sometime after my neck surgery my left arm became flaccid and was totally useless. I also lost a lot of muscle mass throughout my entire body. I needed help for everything I did. I could not even wipe my own ass after I took a shit. I needed help taking a shower (sitting down) and help to dress. I was severely handicapped and it took a long time for me to regain some of these functions and to give my wife some relief. (*)

I still have the ataxic gait, problems with my balance, and mental issues as I was diagnosed with PTSD and other neurological disorders. I'm still waiting for treatment for these illnesses.

I constantly live in fear of the possible doings of my sentencing judge or the involvement of the persecutor. <u>How much more do they want me to suffer for being an innocent person?</u> Not only did I spend time in a penal institution and obtained chronic conditions and illness as a result, but I am also held to the confines of the parole requirements that are far and above those of others with more serious offenses in the same genre who receive lesser time not only for the offense but also for parole. I am on parole for the rest of my life! This is the same thing as a <u>death sentence</u>. And I wonder why I now suffer from high anxiety and depression!

(*) THE WORST THING that was done was not to me but to that of a very innocent person. They sentenced me to a life of hell but they also sentenced my wife to a similar fate and this is totally egregious. I've been married to this woman for over 50 years, and the way I went into this evil system, I came out a different man. At times, I can be very inhospitable and hard to deal with and I know this as I have tried to stop myself, but I am unable. The forces behind these inhospitable actions are currently uncontrollable. This is just another addition on to my egregious sentence which I must suffer, but the worst part of all is my wife has to take the brunt of my hostile actions, and she is not deserving. (*) You think that the court judge, persecutor or my lousy attorney appointed by the sentencing judge really care? I think not. I know not. They apparently can care less.

With all the errors that have been made by the injustice Department, one would think that there would be some form of compassion. But the thought of the word compassion in the injustice Department is quite laughable. (*)

This brings me to the reason why I wrote this book. I know that it will not do anything for me. Writing this book will not help my mental illnesses, but makes it worse; as I write these words of truth it causes me great mental anguish resulting in many trauma attacks. I will absorb these as part of the goal I have set for myself. The purpose is for educating others who are in a similar fate and suffering such as I. The system is broken. The United States has one of the worst incarceration rates compared to that of the rest of the world. The system has gotten to be so bad that it is the laughingstock of the rest of the world. We are no longer a nation of laws but a nation of self-serving politicians who make rules and regulations to satisfy some of their more radical constituents. They have lost the courage and ability to determine right from wrong. They need to fill their pockets with cash. Also behind the scenes are the so-called elitists who do not know what they are talking about but have a microphone to spew there hate and guile. Then there are the wealthy, some of whom are not of this country but who create avenues for disruption and to use their own political views. They have hypnotized their toy soldiers in attacking society for their puppet master. We know who they are, but will anybody do anything about it? NO, as they are fearful of repercussions. (*)

I could go on and on about the brutal sentence and the life I am existing, but I think you get the drift.

Be your own person; be what you are, you are. Don't follow the bass drum to the tune of the puppet master. Take time to think, because I had several years that I was just doing nothing but thinking, and when you realize something, you will see the ugliness in what is transpiring today. This was once a great country, but somehow it has lost its footing and others somehow have the control and they are using the tools of mind control to achieve their sordid agenda. **Be not one of those, be unto yourself.** (*)

It does not have to be, it isn't what it is, but it must be what it should and shall be.

There is No Life after Prison – Only Dispair

• • •

THE TITLE OF THIS CHAPTER is not only depressing, but very true. In my case, it is much more severe because of the conditions placed upon me. But others also suffer a similar fate and I will discuss that first before discussing my fate which is quite depressing as my future is nonexistent. (*)

Those who are released from incarceration are bound to go on parole, which has nuances of what they must do during a certain period of time. Most of these individuals have drug convictions; they must report for drug testing. Some of these drug tests are scheduled while others can be impromptu and at any time in the day or night. If one is dirty (shows drugs in the body), that person can be chastised and given another chance or two, but mostly will end up back in prison again for about one year and one day as that is usually the norm. Other items such as nonpayment of child support can also send them back to prison, where it's impossible for them to pay any support at all. There is then no way that this man can pay the child support, and who suffers the most? It certainly is not the person incarcerated, but it is his family that are the losers. They lose his income generation, and that is if he can find any work which is almost an impossibility. If you have a record of being incarcerated, the chances of your getting a job and keeping that job are realistically nonexistent. And if anybody tells you anything different, please tell them for me that they are full of shit. Many people do not understand that a former inmate is a persona non-grata. The family also loses discipline and the fatherly guidance that he brings to the family. The country loses because of this person's lack of productivity and contributing factors to the economy. **We are all losers for those that are incarcerated.** (*)

Now do not misunderstand me. There are those that need to be put behind bars, and some never should be set free because they are really bad people and no amount of rehabilitation will ever change them into being productive members of society. **And there's a lot of these within the prison today as I met some of them and even got to know some of them and I was not really impressed. We can do well on the outside, but they carried the stigmata that prevents them from ever being successful. However, I do have a solution for them which is included in one of my chapters in this book. Here they can become very successful. They can fail but, then again, it is all up to them to succeed. But they will need your love, your trust, your help and most of all your encouragement and all of you CAN BE WINNERS.** (*)

But on the other hand, there are many others that are incarcerated who could be productive members of society if they found another technique by which they could pay their dues to society. Another form of "punishment" needs to be found, so that these men can support their families and be a positive influence upon others as well as being productive and contributing members of society. We seem to be focusing on the wrong things and need a radical change.

My Case:

My case is totally different from the above. I had a very active business in which I was selling products made in the United States of America. My selling effort supported many families, and some suffer because of my internment. It is such a shame.

I know my wife of now 50 years and how hard she fought for me. I am so blessed to have her by my side and each day I thank God for her. God bless her.

I did not receive proper medical treatment and this is a direct cause of why I am very ill. It is costing taxpayers money and at greater expense than would have happened if I was treated properly within the BOP. Shame on them and those that were there. (*)

I cannot defend my innocence, as I was destined by this court to spend a long time incarcerated and for them to ruin the rest of my life. They would never listen to me, because I believe they have a prejudicial attitude towards me, which makes them blind. (*)

I cannot travel anywhere because of the regulations they have placed upon me such as I can only travel within a certain area and if I am to be in a place for more than three days I have to sign up with the local sheriff as a sex offender. Yes, the innocent must sign up as a sex offender, while, in reality, I am not one.

If I am to sign up while I am at a relative's home it puts them in danger, as I am in danger now from the crazies that come around and do nasty things. I refuse to put anybody in jeopardy, especially family and friends. I will live in my prison without bars as I will not kowtow to some ridiculous rules that have been contrived by some supercilious people. There are those however who need this recognition, but in employing their one-size-fits-all case structure I feel the great fathers of our country are grunting in disdain in their graves. (*)

I have seen people throwing rocks at my house. I was attacked by a man in a supermarket who came at me with his shopping cart and banged into my knee on purpose as I was sitting in a motorized handicapped shopping cart. I cannot defend myself because I cannot carry a gun. What if they were to break into my home to seek some type of crazy thing, such as hurt or kill us. (*)

The government, my government, has figuratively put me on a wanted poster. When will it be put it in the post office? Will that make you happy? All of my friends have left me except for a few very special people. They want nothing to do with me anymore; that really hurts. It hurts really bad. Those who put me there do not understand what the hell and the torture is that I have been submitted to by their pompous actions. They are the Lord thy God and thou shalt kneel before them as they are omnipotent and all-powerful.

Do I seem a bit embittered? Hell, yes, I am! Would you not be? And I have to suffer this way for the rest of my natural life as a directive from the omnipotent court. It is no wonder that I have some mental problems, as they are the purveyor and the maker of my current condition. They should pay for this, but they are immune. Let them go on to the next one who is innocent and damn him to an unmerciful life for as long as he shall live.

I am going to try to live as long as I can so that I will always be a reminder to their past evil deeds. (*)
                              It is what it is

My Prison without Bars

• • •

AFTER SPENDING SEVERAL YEARS IN a federal prison, I come home to my wonderful wife, who cares for me, and takes care of me. Being handicapped was a gracious gift forced upon me by the BOP, due to their lack of proper and timely medical care not only for me, but many others who suffer. I entered this deplorable institution walking and left in a wheelchair with a trunk full of illnesses that I tried to get resolved while I was incarcerated, but to no avail.

Going home was a great and wonderful event. As time moved forward, my illness reached a critical stage and needed immediate attention. **As one problem was resolved, another took its place that was related to the initial illness and was never treated within the BOP. The second illness was more devastating than the first one. If that's not enough, I had a third illness called C. diff (clostridium difficile infection) which if not treated properly could cause death.**

I was in desperate need of a neck operation, and if I did not receive this operation in a very timely manner, I was told I would lose my ability to walk. Thank you, BOP, for now making my life fucking miserable. After the operation for the neck I somehow lost over 50% of my strength plus my left arm became flaccid. I could do nothing with my arm, and I totally relied on my right arm for eating, drinking, trying to clothe myself and even trying to wipe my ass after a bowel movement. I was helpless. I was helpless, and my wife took care of me, giving me showers, dressing me, cleaning up my ass and even feeding me, as I could do none of the items of which I spoke.

During this time of drastic illness and convalescing, I started doing research on the book that I wanted to write while I was incarcerated. I promised myself that I would complete this book, or books, if necessary, telling of my tragic and morbid experiences. It was not a labor of love. In fact, it was a very difficult thing to write and brought back memories that I wish I could forget but never will.

During my research, I found out that I was a slave and am not a free man, but chattel of the government of the United States. This was extremely depressing, and even today depresses me as I write this discussion to you. One cannot imagine the power of rejection by one's country that he loves, and to know this will remain for the rest of his life.

If this is not enough, I must kowtow to certain regulations as imposed on me being a felon. Also, taken away is my right to vote. Ownership of a gun is prohibited; I cannot have any to protect my family from those weirdos who wish to do me harm, because my name is plastered all over the Internet along with my address. And yes, there have been incidences in which these crazies have made known their possible future intent and I have no means of protecting my wife.

If I am to travel and be at the same place for over three days, I have to register with the local sheriff, possibly embarrassing the people that I stayed with, so the solution is simple, I do not visit them, nor will I ever. So, I just stay at home, just as if I am on home confinement.

I am always on the watch for these weirdos and others who would like to do me harm, because if they are looking to do me harm, possibly my wife would be in the line of fire and this is evil. When Congress made these laws regarding this position, their heads must have been totally up their ass. As Congress often does, they make laws without looking at unintended consequences or even more so they are trying to satisfy some small subgroup for their vote. With this unconscionable act, Congress has punished an innocent person. Because of the life, I have to live now and needing assistance from my wife, they have put her in harm's way and are punishing her for helping me. This is all very sad as there are no words that I can use to express my distaste to you. **You, in my book, have sunk to the lowest of the low, and even the devil is ten steps over your hand in integrity. SHAME ON YOU.**

I do not drive because of my illnesses, therefore depend upon my wife to take me everywhere. This is another burden on her as there is nothing I can do about it.

I cannot work, because I don't have the strength. The injustice Department sent me to the BOP with purposeful forethought knowing that I would not get the proper medical treatment that I would need. And why? MONEY.

The injustice Department has completed part of its quota for new initiates to the BOP, and the BOP runs its medical system under the guidelines of minimalism. Minimalism medical care is just giving its charges only what is necessary to keep them alive. The less the better.

So, I sit here writing this book to you and you must understand that from my time within the BOP, I garnered another illness of which I have yet to receive treatment, that being PTSD. You may say that this illness PTSD is only contracted by those who serve in the Armed Forces, but you are so wrong. In speaking with psychologists and sociologists, I have been told that usually geriatric inmates readily garner this disease, and if you are innocent, PTSD is most often the certainty.

I may be without physical bars, but my bars are mental **and affect my freedom by which** I relive every single day the horrors of my past.

I wish there were a way by which I could let you have my mind just for a couple hours and let me watch, for I will see you scream in terror and want to be relieved of this affliction. **And that is why I live in a prison without bars.**

It is what it is

Federal Bureau of Investigation

• • •

THE FEDERAL BUREAU OF INVESTIGATION or the FBI is the police force of the federal government, and its history shows they have been agents for the President of the United States.

If you ever should have a visit from the FBI, I caution you, do not be alone. I was alone and they will twist your words. They play bad cop good cop and will put you in positions that there is no right answer and any answer you give will be used against you even as it seems innocent at the time. Do not let them into your house or business if it has to do with you. Make sure you have your attorney there present with you when talking to them. If you do not have an attorney nor do not really want one, what you need is to go pro se and tell them such, and the courts will have to determine what to do. But this gives you time to get over the shock value that is induced by their presence.

When they first approach you, insist they show you their badges; you will be deeply shocked. How do I know this? Experience, my dear readers, experience. I have been there so I can speak with some experience, or maybe a lot of experience.

Some of my words and comments have been twisted and they used terms to their advantage and said things that were not really true. I was upset and went to find out what was going on with these innuendos they made. The FBI apparently does lie and are trained to lie. But if you lie, that is a felony offense, and you can be prosecuted. I asked the same question of my attorney, and received the same answer. (*)

It appears that their job is to get anything out of you so they could convict you or even appear to convict you. You do not have a chance at all. The only chance that you have is not to speak to them at any time. Silence is your answer to questions of the FBI. Otherwise, you are doomed.

If you have a story to tell, tell your story factually one time, and one time only and if they ask questions about your story do not answer them, because that's where the twisting and turning just starts. (*)

I always considered the FBI to be my friend, but now I am very wary of their presence. I will not speak to them.

This chapter was just to warn you of potential damage to you that could come if questioned by the FBI. I'm not saying that it's all bad, that is wrong. But I must admit to you that they are very well trained in what they do and if their scope of investigation is upon you, you can be certain that they will become extremely vigilant and very tenacious in putting you away by any means necessary. I have heard too many stories while incarcerated of the antics that they do play.

It is what it is

United States Marshal

• • •

THE UNITED STATES MARSHAL'S OFFICE is to protect the staff and employees of the Justice Department such as the federal court offices.

They have a secondary function which is that of transporting prisoners from one facility to another, to court and on leaves of absence granted by the BOP for extenuating circumstances of family, which is extremely rare.

When I was transported within my own area, I was treated roughly, especially given my unhealthy condition. My hands and feet were shackled and I had a difficult time with my balance and was told to get in a van unassisted. I could not get into the van when one of these genteel Marshall's pushed me from behind and shoved me face-first into a seat knocking my glasses off and causing some cuts on my face. Did they care? HELL NO.

I had to be transported from my point of origin, or home base, to a holding facility where they would define in which institution I was to reside and would stay there until such judgment had been made and then finally taken there by a Con Air.

I had the distinct privilege of taking Con Air several times. The plane is an old, and I mean old, L1011. If you are not familiar with this plane, it was built many years ago by Lockheed for use in public transportation, and I flew the aircraft once in the private sector, promising never to fly that aircraft again.

Now I was being transported to another facility in this 30-year-old aircraft that I worried had minimal if any maintenance whatsoever. As I looked out over the wing I saw patches of duct tape holding the wing together. The inside sounds are those of worn-out bearings that run the equipment. Now I do understand how expendable we are.

It is what it is

Many Agree with Me

• • •

AN OFFICIAL WITHIN THE JUSTICE Department made reference to the fact that I was charged, sentenced and convicted for what I MIGHT do.

Thank you on hold.

I was informed by other officials within the government that I had been screwed. (*)

There are quite a few people inside the confines of the judicial department that know my plight and there is not a thing that they can do about it, nor can I. The rest of my life has been destroyed, and I live in a prison without bars. Forever I'll be shackled by invisible handcuffs and leg irons, always looking over my shoulder for the FBI to recur and possibly take me away from whence I shall never be heard from or seen again. You asked if this is done? YES. They call this dieseling, where they take you from one facility to another and you stay there for a short period of time in confinement and then go on to the next facility until you eventually die and they put you in this plain box and bury you along with others who never made it out alive. (*)

It is what it is

The Naked Truth

• • •

WHAT YOU READ IN THIS book you might feel or believe is just not possible, especially in the caregiving and compassionate country that we live within known as The United States of America. My dear reader, if you believe that, your eyes are closed and you live in a cognitive stupor. I am not going to get political, but you need to open your eyes if you have not. So, what I say and write to you is "THE NAKED TRUTH."

This bastardized, evil and demonic adventure will be told in the actual vernacular, so you may not like some of the things that are said or how they are said, but "it is, what it is". The saying," it is, what it is" was spoken often while I was incarcerated. This gives you an insight into what and how an inmate has to think to survive. It is a sign of despair which is very prevalent. There is no looking for moral justifications or absolution from their crimes, but just an attitude for survival. They are nothing more than captive animals and treated as such.

On February 11, 2017 President Trump stated that "the justice system is broken". My survival cements his statement.

I have written this dissertation not to please anyone including myself nor to make any political statements but to state emphatically the terror and the trauma I experienced within the judicial system. I am only one case as there are many more who have been wronged. But, there are also some of the nastiest people behind bars and in my estimation, they should never be set free. (*)

I fear consequences as I write this disastrous story. The emissaries of the Department of Injustice DOI, (my name for the Department of Justice or DOJ) could easily pick me up without any protocol as you have rights and I do not. They can pick me up and send me out never to be seen or heard from again to die in some gruesome, lonesome cell because I dared speak the truth. (*) I fear not that they want to punish me again, because I must bring out the truth and the truth shall be known. I fear them not.

I am only one of the hundreds of thousands who have their own tragic story, and that number is growing at a rapid rate with more prisons being built and taxpayers' money being wasted and squandered and with profiteering by some, as "it is all about the 'MONEY'. And that is the NAKED TRUTH.

Before I go too much further I have to tell you something about my regressing health which was exacerbated by the Department of injustice, how I proceeded through the network to get convicted, and then was placed within the penal institution where timely and proper medical care was literally absent. I came home a broken man. I suffer from PTSD. I can hear you saying you cannot get PTSD from anyplace else except from being in a war zone, and you are so wrong. Go look it up.

Sociologists and psychologists have told me that is not unusual for someone who is incarcerated, and especially for an elderly person, to get PTSD and it is even more predominant when that person is innocent. I also suffer from tremors which is a physiological manifestation that something is wrong with my body. But this is only part of it. There is the deliberate lack of timely and proper medical care, the burglary (yes, I did say burglary), the retaliation by some of the staff at federal institution or by the person I believe that set me up, taking advantage not only of a geriatric man but also of his geriatric wife. The sinfulness of this act cannot be excused by confession. I shan't hunt you down, because I am not a violent man that would beget violence.

I'm having a difficult time writing this book because of the terrors that my soul, my body and my being are reliving in this nightmare every day and night as the flash-backs are horrible and I relive again the horror, especially within the Federal court. This is a chapter unto itself.

The brutality of mankind is enormous, and the compassion of the multitude is even far greater. The brutality of these people is beyond one's scope of reality unless you have lived through this trauma. One needs to try to understand how cruel and what pompous asses they are. They treat you like servile underlings and look down upon you with scorn. This has the distinct odor of the feudal system as we are the serfs and we kowtow to the Master.

I digress… I at times cannot help myself, as you cannot help yourself under certain circumstances because you know you have been alienated, cast aside, even shunned or some other adjective that I cannot quite comprehend at this time.

If you do not like what I am saying, simply throw the book away, or better yet, give it to a friend.

It is what it is

(*) Author considers significant

Why Me?

• • •

WHY ME? THIS PHRASE KEEPS reoccurring many times during the week even today. I still don't understand how I was placed in this situation except for my supposition that I was set up.

I was going to write an eloquent closing statement, but the more I thought about it, I did not feel it necessary. Because you my dear readers if you have read this book, there is nothing more than I can tell you. You know everything about me is I have bared my soul.

I have an old saying that people go through life seeing but their eyes are closed. I hope that this book may have opened your eyes but maybe you can see some truth. I give you some starting points for what to look for but it is not for me to direct your life, it is up to you.

Educate yourself, look beyond what is there, because we are held within the guise of many falsehoods, that you do not see, but it is there and real.

It is not as it should be

Check Your Prescription Medication Anomalies

• • •

IT IS A KNOWN FACT that certain medications can cause you to do things that you would not normally do. It could cause you to be put in a position whereby you could violate a crime and with the amount of crimes that are on the books, anything can happen.

You would think that the injustice system would be savvy enough to look at these anomalies, but they simply want to fry your ass. After I was released I found that the persecutor had used several different studies, which were proven to be bogus, wrong and improperly taken, but nonetheless he used them as empirical fact.

Then remember dear readers it is five against you, and if you are locked up in jail awaiting your sentence or your trial, you have to rely upon your attorney, and many times he is a friend of the court, just like mine, and his goal is to get a plea.

So if you are taking medications make sure that you investigate them deeply as to what adverse effects there are, as many are hidden from the population so you have to look deep. I suggest you look to the Mayo Clinic's analysis.

Remember one thing, their job is to put you in jail.
It is what it is

CONCLUSION - THE BOMBSHELL

• • •

AFTER MY RESEARCH AND FINDING the incompetency and unknowledgeable state of this court, my case should have been thrown out immediately. My rights have been extremely violated, and what would be done about it – NOTHING. I had to suffer an unjustifiable punishment for something in which I had no involvement in any way shape or form.

I firmly believe that the court, including my so-called attorney, does not give a damn; just send them off to jail and the court jumps at the strings of the puppet master who is the abominable sentencing commission.

It was in my recent visit to the Mayo Clinic that highlights of the incompetency of our current broken court system is not recognizing adverse effects of medication upon a person.

The judge should have found the answer doing Men's Rae, which I believe he did not even attempt. With his tunnel-vision the super steroidal prosecutor cares not for justice, but only for his maintenance of his batting record and gives incorrect data in court.

As for my attorney, nothing from this idiot. The only goal in his life is to collect the monies that they are supposedly paying for defending their clients, how much it costs for his children to go to this expensive Catholic school, and from my experience has a total lack of any ability to defend his client in court.

Yes, I do have the reason why. Medical, for many reasons.

Bring the poor innocent slobs in to go through the motions of getting an attempt at justice, then give them JusXtice and send them off to prison.

THANK YOU TO MY WONDERFUL READERS

• • •

I AM NOT THAT NAÏVE as to think that some of you will read this book and will not totally agree with me. That's fine. We just have our brains wired differently, that's all. But there's one thing you cannot dispel, and that is the truth. And sometimes if you're not careful, it can choke you.

Those that have read the entire manuscript, I am damn proud of you. It is not a pretty read, but a real need. I had a difficult time writing it, because I had to relive some of the things over and over again to get the words on paper; you know how it is done.

This book is the most difficult to write. The second book will be a lot easier, and I daresay may be more humorous also, because I have some anecdotes and stories to tell, and like this book, it is all factual.

Somehow, I think the Lord has kept me alive to write this book and hopefully the next.

As I thank you for reading this book, I also thank my wife and she has been so supportive, and some friends, two of my brothers, a fraternity brother and of course our "sister "across the pond in Italy.

There are also a number of other people I would like to thank: former inmate friends, including two who needlessly died a horrible death in prison.

REMEMBER:
THE LAW IS MADE FOR THEM.
You will understand this more if you read some of the books I have suggested in the appendix, especially the ones on the committee of 300, because if today you are blind, after you read, you shall see, understand and be enlightened.

Thank you
Iam Clarize

MOST OF ALL. I THANK GOD FOR GIVING ME THE COURAGE, WISDOM, HEALTH AND TENACITY TO WRITE THIS BOOK AS IT NEEDS TO BE WRITTEN AND DISCUSSED. HE HAS TRULY BLESSED ME IN MANY WAYS.

I WILL HAVE A WEBSITE WITH SOME OF MY WRITINGS PLACED THERE.
SOME OF MY WRITINGS MAY OPEN YOUR EYES.

I am not done yet. Visit my websites
www.iamclarize.com
www.jusxtice.com
emails:
IC@iamclarize.com
JX@jusxtice.com

Do not expect me to be on any social media platforms, as they are a waste of time and are not productive. If you need to talk to me, email me with your telephone number and the reason for your call and I will contact you. And as for you haters, go someplace else as I will not bother with you.

Thank you and God Bless.

Iam Clarize

EDUCATIONAL SOURCES

• • •

IF YOU ARE INTERESTED IN knowing more about mind control, being locked up for the first time and about a very eye-opening form of mind control that is not for the faint of heart, I recommend the following book as an excellent start into understanding the nuances of mind control. This is an easy to read book which explains a lot about the different types of mind control and how we are all affected. It is part of our daily lives so I suggest that you take a look into the subject. The book's title is:
Mind Control 101 by Dantalion Jones

I recommend viewing the series:
Locked Up: First Timers
This TV series highlights the culture shock of prison life from the perspective of the recently arrived, including teens, drug addicts and a former cop.
This documentary is available on Netflix and also on YouTube and I would not suggest that children under the age of 14 watch it.

This film is available on Amazon, and I recommend those who are faint of heart or those under the age of 18 do not watch this film. I admit, it is quite ugly. I do not necessarily recommend this for viewing, but felt the necessity that you know it is available:

American Mind Control: MK Ultra

Project MK Ultra was formed by the CIA who drugged, raped, tortured and murdered innocent citizens when, after WWII, the US extracted Nazi scientists to perform top secret testing on human subjects. MK Ultra was reportedly shut down, but experts reveal it's very much alive today.

Starring:
Bill Pitt, Paul Hughes, John Roberson
Runtime:
1 hour, 4 minutes

EXCELLENT BOOK
Three Felonies A Day: How the Feds Target the Innocent (Paperback – June 7, 2011)
by Harvey Silverglate (Author),
Alan M. Dershowitz (Foreword)

The Conspirators Hierarchy
the Committee of 300
by Dr. John Coleman

Conspirators Hierarchy:
the Story of the Committee of 300
by Dr. John Coleman

Global Compass – Prison: Break filmed in conjunction with The Economist FILMS @2015

From these suggestions, you may now desire to start your Internet research as it contains all the information you need.

It is what it is

www.ingramcontent.com/pod-product-compliance
Lightning Source LLC
Chambersburg PA
CBHW050202230526
45470CB00001B/205